SURVIVING GROUP MEETINGS

SURVIVING GROUP MEETINGS
Practical Tools for Working in Groups

LARRY POWELL
JOELENE SMITH VICKERS
JONATHAN AMSBARY
MARK HICKSON III

BrownWalker Press
Boca Raton

Surviving Group Meetings: Practical Tools for Working in Groups

BrownWalker Press
Boca Raton, Florida • USA
2009

ISBN-10: 1-59942-521-1 *(paper)*
ISBN-13: 978-1-59942-521-4 *(paper)*

ISBN-10: 1-59942-522-X *(ebook)*
ISBN-13: 978-1-59942-522-1 *(ebook)*

www.brownwalker.com

Library of Congress Cataloging-in-Publication Data

Surviving group meetings : practical tools for working in groups /
Larry Powell ... [et al.].
  p. cm.
Includes bibliographical references.
ISBN-13: 978-1-59942-521-4 (pbk. : alk. paper)
ISBN-10: 1-59942-521-1 (pbk. : alk. paper)
1. Business communication. 2. Meetings. 3. Public speaking. I.
Powell, James Larry, 1948- II. Title.

HF5718.S87 2009
658.4'56--dc22

2009042115

Contents

PREFACE

We have become a nation of meetings.

Organizations call meetings to make corporate decisions, plan marketing strategies, make personnel decisions, and to engage in a myriad of other activities that—far too often—seem utterly useless to its participants.

Sometimes meetings drag on for hours, leaving most of the participants wondering when or if it will ever end. Frequently the group's members will labor over a decision, spending dozens of hours, only to see their recommendations overruled or dismissed. Other decisions are made by committees and never implemented by the organization.

These frustrations are not limited to the work environment. Civic clubs, churches, athletic teams, and volunteer organizations will find that much of their time is spent in meetings. Some groups will spend more time meeting and discussing their goals and purposes than they will actually use in carrying out those same goals.

Meanwhile the number of labor hours devoted to group activities seems to be increasing. Our corporate fascination with the group process has expanded into more and more areas. Decisions that—twenty years ago—were made by individuals in position of responsibility are now delegated to committees.

The goal of such changes is admirable. By obtaining committee input on personnel decisions, an autocratic tyrannical manager cannot abuse his or her position. Marketing decisions will go through a more thoughtful process, reducing the likelihood of spending millions of dollars on a product that won't sell. Groups are, in essence, a safety net that hope to ensure both fairness and thoroughness in the decision making process.

The reality of modern life, though, is that group meetings are starting to expand and limit the productivity of the modern organization. In some organizations, the trend has become so strong that they now declare "meeting-free days," designating one day per week when no meetings are allowed. The practice is necessary to let management workers catch up on their e-mails and respond to the myriad of paperwork that can drown the efficiency of an organization.

In such an environment, we hope to offer a fresh look at the group process. We do not view group meetings as inherently good or bad—merely necessary. Our intent is to provide the reader with an understanding of the group processes with the hope that such knowledge will increase one's proficiency in that process.

If meetings have to occur, we should at least learn how to survive them. Involved within the concept of "surviving meetings," though, are several concepts. We hope to approach each of these in various parts of the book.

Surviving meetings means making the group meeting a successful one. The first focus should be on solving the problem faced by the group. If that becomes the group's priority, it can often be achieved in a relatively short time. The group is successful and the meeting is completed. You've survived round one, knowing—of course—that others will follow.

Surviving meetings means the group itself continues to exist. For the individual to be successful, the group must be successful. For the individual to continue in the relationship, the group must continue to exist. In social situations, the priority of this element may vary. In the work environment, though, the ability to survive meetings in this manner may mean the difference between keeping or losing a job. The company that goes bankrupt has few happy workers.

Surviving meetings means that the rights of you, the individual, have been protected. The time of company loyalty to its workers seems to be passing. After decades in which group processes have focused on ideal collaborative efforts, the academic community is finally beginning to realize that too much collaboration is like too much accommodation—somebody gets taken. In today's work environment, individuals and groups must be willing to assert their legitimate rights. Such actions are often essential for the individual to continue to be a member of that group.

Surviving meetings can also mean simply making it through the process. For many people, the common interpretation of that phrase is that they simply hope the meeting ends soon. We share your hope, but we ask that it not end too soon. Learn how to get through the meeting and address its issues as effectively as possible. Make it through the process by completing the process.

Then you have survived the meeting. Another one down. Several thousand still to go.

CHAPTER 1

INTRODUCTION:
MEETINGS AS A NECESSARY EVIL

Today's America is perhaps the hardest working and most productive society in the history of the world. More people are working than ever before. They work in retail, service industries, in cyberspace, in industry, and on farms. Americans put at least eight hours a day into making a living. For the most part, this hard work has been a result of more efficient work. Because of computers, writers no longer have to re-write an entire page to correct a single typographical error. It doesn't take two people, a writer and a typist, to correct a page. Farmers no longer hoe fields manually. Industrial workers no longer assemble automobiles piece by piece. And, just as automated fruit pickers and computers have increased our levels of productivity, so has efficient thinking.

The Essential Nature of Meetings

Today's highly productive world also requires many meetings, especially for white collar workers. When a book editor signs an author to a contract, there must be meetings with the senior editor. Sometimes there is a meeting with the Vice President or the President of the company. Surveys repeatedly show mid-level managers spend anywhere from 25-to-60 percent of their time in meetings. Top management spends as much as four of every five working days in meetings (Lang, 1999). Unfortunately, this does not even include the time one spends at home, in planes, or in cars, preparing for a meeting.

Certainly there is no problem with having meetings, per se. However, there are "practice" meetings for the "real" meetings. Employees want to ensure that they avoid embarrassment and that their viewpoints receive a vote of approval after all is said and done. The problem with all of these meetings, however, is that—in most instances—more is said than is done. Sometimes participants in meetings sit around and wait for 15-20 minutes while someone goes to a copy machine because there were not enough copies of a report, or the one "expert" in the company was not invited to the meeting. Some participants are interrupted by others because the others are seeking out criticisms before hearing an entire report. Some reports take too long. In short, we are not having efficient meetings, and we are having too many of them. The 3M Company (Minnesota Mining and Manufacturing) surveyed 2,800 managers in business, academia, and government and found that 40 percent of them believe that one quarter to one-half of all of the time spent in meetings is wasted (Lang, 1999).

Using conservative numbers, then, twenty-five percent of the work week is spent in meetings. That is ten hours per week. Of that ten hours, forty percent of the time is wasted according to the 3M sample. That is four hours of wasted time. Multiply that by an average of 10 persons attending a meeting. That means that one full position, at a conservative salary of $50,000, is wasted for each and every group that has such meetings. At a conservative estimate of 10,000 organizations in the United States, that means we are wasting a half million dollars a year. Considering the number is closer to 100,000 organizations, then it's probably closer to half a *billion* dollars a year. That is the conservative figure. A more realistic figure has been provided by Kayser (1990) who claimed that $37 billion per year is wasted due to poor meeting management. Kayser's figures, too, are probably conservative in that they are close to 20 years old. Still, the numbers are staggering. But the question on an individual level is what could one get done with an extra four hours per week.

Generally, while people value the opportunity to work productively with others, they dislike the reality of meetings. Typical complaints about meetings include unclear objectives, inadequate preparation of leader and members, lengthy meetings, information overload, discussions monopolized by one or two members, digressive talk, rehashing of old issues, personal agendas, no follow-up of decisions, and games of verbal volleyball.

Even though many meetings are filled with problems, some group members have indicated that there are positive outcomes. The managers surveyed by 3M reported, that despite the time wasted, their meetings were for the most part, rated on the "productive" side. There is hope for fruitful collaboration to emerge from meetings. Meetings are a reality of modern organizations, and group communication is inevitable whether on the job or in our personal lives. Nevertheless negotiating within a group can be like maneuvering through a mine field at times.

As we maneuver through this book, we will outline and discuss means by which some of the problems involved in group meetings can be alleviated, or at least diminished. In this first chapter, we will outline a few of the difficulties that are discussed by the 3M survey sample as well as by others. In brief form, we will illustrate how some solutions are possible.

Factors Contributing to Negative Attitudes About Meetings

As the 3M survey indicates, several factors cause some people to feel that their time has been wasted in meetings. Individuals may have different reasons, depending on the personalities of all of the members involved, the nature of the group, the problem at hand, and the amount of time expended. However, we have tried to categorize the general types of difficulties.

Difficulty One: Preparing for the Meeting

Several of the items mentioned by the 3M group indicate that there is often a lack of planning for meetings. Obviously, planning can mean a number of different things. For example, it may mean that some people didn't bring pencil and paper. It may mean that some people were not in the right "frame of mind" to carry on a meeting. It may mean that the leader did not provide enough pre-meeting information for the members to know what would be discussed. It may mean that there was not enough time to cover the material, or that there was too much time to cover so few issues.

As we discuss preparation, though, we should be careful to remember what the 3M people said. That is, leaders and members are often unprepared. When a report is left behind in another office (or worst yet, another city), the number of person-hours wasted is high. When some members are late arriving, similar problems occur. Consideration needs to be paid to who needs to be at the meeting, that all necessary materials are there, that the environment (heating, air conditioning, freedom from noise, the absence of interruptions, etc.) is pleasant, that group members are seated comfortably (but not too comfortably). Further, the members should be aware of the topic and the type of meeting. For example, is it a *precursory meeting* in which the members are there to meet one another (to introduce everyone to the "team"? Is it merely an *exploratory meeting*, where they are trying to come up with many suggestions without doing much evaluation? It is an *implementation meeting*, where they are seeking methods to utilize a solution that has already been found? Is it a *problem-solving meeting* in which all members participate in defining the problem as well as possible solution? Is it a *decision-making meeting* in which several solutions have been brought to the table and the function of the group is to choose one or more of them?

Unfortunately, many leaders and members never consider what kind of meeting they are attending until the meeting is in progress. When this happens some members leave the meeting disappointed because the meeting never got to the phase for which they were most prepared. In addition, each member should be appraised of any documents that need to be read prior to the meeting. Otherwise, eight people may be sitting around, with each one reading the document, in which case the preparation occurs during the meeting instead of before the meeting. Another typical problem in meeting preparation is that some critical member has not been invited. It may be that sometimes people are invited who will have no input, but that is much less wasteful than waiting for 15 minutes to find the "lost expert." These are but a few of the preparation problems that will be discussed in more detail later in this book.

Difficulty Two: Quantity and Quality of Talk

Another problem is the quality and quantity of talk by each member. There are cases where one member simply has more information than some others do. The complaints of group members, however, are usually not about information. The complaints are about the quality and quantity of talk. Some people simply take 15 minutes to say what could (and should) be said in three minutes. Because the other members do not want to be rude, they allow the excessive talker to drone on and on. After the meeting they resent this person. In other cases, two group members get into a fray over a side issue about which the other members are disinterested. Getting off the topic is a regular complaint about meetings (Arbuckle & Nohara-LeClair, 2000). In addition, some members are concerned about re-hashing information that has been previously discussed.

Difficulty Three: Personal Agendas

At some meetings there are members who feel they are in competition with one another, sometimes for resources and at other times
simply for attention. Others may view the meeting as a chance to
enhance their personal image with the group, sometimes at the expense of others (Schlenker & Weigold, 1992). Others may have an
underlying goal that influences their behavior (Plaks, Shafer & Shoda, 2003). They get into arguments which affect not only their relationships with one another and with the other members of the group
but also with the group as an entity. Sometimes these personal agendas are obvious and at other times they are more covert. For example, one member may disagree with an analysis of a problem or a
solution to be a problem simply because it came from a particular
person. In the worst possible case, you may have the other members
"siding up" with one side or the other. The important aspect of this
is not only the lack of compatibility created by such a distortion, but
bad decision-making based on inadequate or inaccurate information.

Difficulty Four: Information Overload

As we have already mentioned, there should be a correlation between
the purpose of the meeting, the agenda, the members invited, and
the amount of time to resolve the issue(s). If members of a company
were discussing whether to build a new office in Washington, DC, it
would probably take less time than deciding how to handle a 100
million dollar lawsuit. When discussing the re-structuring of an organization, substantially more time would enter the conversation
than one about whether to increase production of an item by two
percent. Issues which involve people, especially the hiring or firing of
people, will take longer. It may take even longer if some of the group
members are potential targets of a restructuring. Therefore, we must
take into consideration how much information can be covered given
the amount of time designated for the meeting. Not only do "people
problems" take more time, but also issues which involve evaluation
of substantial statistical data from a variety of sources. The result
may be an information overload that will require breaking the discussion into sub-components that can be spread over several meetings
(Farhoomand & Drury, 2002).

All of us have information overload most of the time (MacDonald & Oettinger, 2002). To understand what a problem it can be,
simply consider taking a two-week vacation. When you return, you
have memoranda to read, reports to read, voice mails and e-mails to

answer. This information applies both to one's corporate life and personal life, and can have a direct impact on decisional quality (Hwang & Lin, 1999). Meetings should be focused toward clarity, not obfuscation.

Difficulty Five: Lack of Follow-Up and Follow-Through

When an individual makes a decision, they can often move toward implementing that decisions themselves. Groups, however, face implementation obstacles that are harder to overcome, because the group's implementation plan often requires actions from individual group members (Knoblich & Jordan, 2003). At some meetings, individuals are assigned a task of generating some data for the next meeting. When members fail to undertake their tasks, then the entire group is at a disadvantage at the subsequent meeting. When the leader fails to implement a decision or solution that has been agreed upon at a meeting, the members begin believing that the meetings themselves are not worthwhile. Even worse, when a group makes a recommendation to someone and never receives any kind of response, group members tend to become frustrated and hostile.

These, then, are some of the typical complaints about meetings. Most people do not mind going to a meeting if they feel that they are going to have an opportunity for involvement and that there is some outcome that has meaning. In short, the basic complaint is that *too many meetings lack meaning*.

Meetings as Alternative Processes

As we all know, much of what goes on at meetings could be sent through an e-mail message. Sometimes two individuals could get together to "hash out" some problem. There are times, though, that meetings with several individuals are needed to make a group work.

Characteristically, most people's perceptions about meetings are derived from their own experiences. As a result, some people have positive feelings about meetings because they have had the good fortune of having leaders who know the methods of conducting meetings. Others are not so fortunate, but because their only knowledge is taken from negative experience, they too, often chair meetings that are not so fruitful. While imitation may work for some things, it is not the best method for learning how to conduct meetings. There is an alternative approach available, however. That approach is to learn what the theorists and educators say, taking full advantage of a number of positive approaches to meetings. The methods in this book are based on those developed almost 40 years ago.

Background for This Book

William Stephen Smith wrote a classic textbook (1965) on how to participate in small group decision making. While there are elements of that text that are as outdated as some of the clothing of the 1960s, there are other aspects of it that hold up today. Three of the authors of this book had Dr. Smith as a mentor. Together, we have tried to blend the positive elements of the traditional approaches to group problem solving with some of the more innovative approaches in today's world.

In that context, the remainder of the book is divided into the following chapters. Chapter Two is about the socialization process, that is, how one becomes a participating member of a group. While all of us have participated in a group at some time, we must become re-socialized in each new group that we join. Chapter Two illustrates that there is a method to this madness. Chapter Three is on interpersonal dynamics in groups. This chapter is devoted to creating positive working relationships. Chapter Four looks at approaches to group problem solving. Several different approaches are discussed about how to organize effective meetings. Chapter Five is about monitoring one's own verbal and nonverbal behavior as well as the behavior of others. Chapter Six discusses evaluation, that is, how the group decides if it has performed well or performed poorly. Such evaluations can benefit the group by making changes for the next meeting. Chapter Seven is built around the concept of negotiation. Chapter Eight is on implementation, that is, evaluating how well the group members actually use these techniques while working. Chapter Nine is on leadership. Because the notion that "All people are created equal" does not seem to apply in many group meetings, we have developed an approach to dealing with power and conflict and their relationship to leadership in the group. The final chapter, Chapter Ten, focuses on maintaining a positive environment for groups to work.

Summary

We know that people are participating in more and more meetings as the society becomes more productive and we know many participants feel that meetings are a waste of time. However, we also know that meetings do not have to be a waste of time. Instead we can learn that group decision making and problem solving involve a process by which those who attend can feel good about the meeting and something can be accomplished at the same time. The remainder of this book is devoted to that goal.

References

Arbuckle, T. Y., & Nohara-LeClair, M. (2000). Effect of off-target verbosity on communication efficiency in a referential communication task. *Psychology & Aging, 15,* 65-77.

Chu, Phillip (2005, May 16). *The art of the meeting.* Huntington Beach, CA: Technicat.

Effective meetings (2005, Feb. 8). Pleasantville, Nova Scotia: Align Learning International

Farhoomand, A. F., & Drury, D. H. (2002). Managerial information overload. *Communications of the ACM, 45(10),* 127-131.

Hwang, M. I., & Lin, J. W. (1999). Information dimension, information overload and decision quality. *Journal of Information Science, 25,* 213-218.

Kayser, T. A. (1990). *Mining group gold.* El Segundo, CA: Serif.

Knoblich, G., & Jordan, J. S. (2003). Action coordination in groups and individuals: Learning anticipatory control. *Journal of Experimental Psychology: Learning, Memory & Cognition, 29,* 1006-1016.

Lang, J. (1999, Mar 27). Meeting the day away: Survey finds wasted time in boardrooms. *Birmingham Post-Herald,* C14.

MacDonald, M. S., & Oettinger, A. G. (2002). Information overload. *Harvard International Review, 24(3),* 44-48.

Plaks, J. E., Shafer, J. L., & Shoda, Y. (2003). Perceiving individuals and groups as coherent: How do perceivers make sense of variable behavior? *Social Cognition, 21,* 26-60.

Schlenker, B. R., & Weigold, M. F. (1992). Interpersonal processes involving impression regulation and management. *Annual Review of Psychology, 4,* 133-168.

Smith, W. S. (1965). *Group problem-solving through discussion: A process essential to democracy.* Indianapolis: Bobbs-Merrill.

Weisert, Conrad (1999, Sept. 5). *Too many conference calls.* Chicago: Information Disciplines, Inc.

SOMETHING TO THINK ABOUT
TOO MANY MEETINGS, TOO LITTLE ACCOMPLISHED

Many people identify with Philip Chu's (2005) complaint that "meetings are evil, and I'm not convinced they're even a necessary evil. I personally don't even enjoy the rare productive meeting, much less the more typical painfully unproductive meetings" (p. 1). His frustration is understandable in today's organizational environment. A typical organizational manager attends an average of 5.3 hours per week, accounting for more than 11 hours of contact time per week. Further, the number seems to be growing, with the increase being of enough concern that some organizations have "meetingless Thursdays" to ensure that their workers will have some allotted time to meet with customers and accomplish their required tasks.

Others see the proliferation of meetings as a sign of problems. Organizational consultant Conrad Weisert (1999) noted "that projects that were 'in trouble' held too many team meetings and most of the meetings were too long. Indeed the weekly or even daily 'status meeting' was a sure indicator of an out-of-control project" (p. 1).

Align Learning identified four reasons meeting can have such a negative impact ("Effective meetings," 2005). These include:

1. *The Warm Body Syndrome.* The people who attend have no specific purpose for being there and are not active participants.
2. *The Cobweb Caucus.* Too many meetings seem to lack a specific focus.
3. *The Headless Horseman.* A lack of leadership on the part of the person conducting the meeting.
4. *The Hot Air Habit.* The meeting produces a lot of talk, but little action.

Have you experienced such problems in any of your recent meetings? Do you believe meetings are generally helpful or generally useless?

CHAPTER 2

THE SOCIALIZATION PROCESS

Just two weeks ago, Juan was hired by Blueplate Industries. He went through a formal process with the human resources people, called *orientation*, on his first day at work. Orientation means introducing the employees to the ways of the organization, but the process generally has become a time for completing forms for medical coverage, listening to policies on leave time, and obtaining an employee identification card.

On the second day, he moved into his new office. On his third day, he began working. Juan had no problem in doing what he had been asked to do. What has been a problem for him is learning to adapt to the new environment, sometimes called a *culture*. Every organization and each office within the organization tends to have its own culture. Moving from being a stranger in the company to becoming part of the company requires that each individual who enters go through the process of *socialization*. For all practical purposes, socialization is the process of learning the culture of the group one is entering so that the newcomer can simultaneously fit into the existing group while developing their individual abilities (Barge & Schlueter, 2004).

A number of communication researchers have indicated that socialization is a three-step process: anticipation, encounter, and identification (Conrad, 1994; Hickson & Stacks, 1998). When one enters college, the anticipation may be that college will be much like high school. All of us tend to move in the direction of behaving as usual. For the most part, then, we treat strange situations all the same. The same is true regarding working in groups. When we enter a new group—whether it is a fraternity, sorority, church, synagogue, or honor society—we tend to behave much the same as we did in previous organizations. The work group may be different though. A work group may be temporary for even a day or two. A work group may last for years. The problem is that we do not always know, in advance, how long it will last. Nevertheless, we need to learn how to function as we go through the stages of anticipation, identification, and encounter.

Anticipation

As a neophyte in the group, a most important task is determining how the group works. Unfortunately, there is usually no one to provide the answer. If someone does give you the answer, it may not be an accurate view, at least not for you. Asking questions about how to act in a group meeting may also be socially inappropriate. Therefore, to some extent, there is trial-and-error involved. The error part needs to be avoided as much as possible.

A first step in anticipation is making an analysis and evaluation of how this group may be similar and different from other groups with which you have worked. For example, in college you may have been assigned group projects. Some instructors even gave group grades for such projects. Even so, the "grade" in this case may be about whether you maintain the job, receive a promotion, or get fired. Thus, the consequences of your work are much greater. In addition, you are always being "graded" in reference to generating embarrassment for yourself. In some instances, embarrassment is a consequence that, for the moment at least, is worse than getting fired.

The Charge to the Group

Most of the time, groups have a "charge." In essence, the **charge** is the mission given to the group by some superior. Most often superiors assign a group to work on something because as individuals they do not want to make decisions, they are unable to make decisions, or both. There are times when such a charge is written. Many times the charge is ambiguous. Most often the charge is worded in such a way that the group's outcome is advisory to the superior. A written charge may be seen as a **formal statement of mission**. In other cases, the charge may come about as a discussion between the superior and the chair of the group. In these cases, the chair may be seen as the "spokesperson" for the superior who is most often absent from group meetings.

In any event, the group must decide what its charge is, based on what has been delivered. For example, if a group is asked to serve as a "search" committee to seek a new director of human relations with a charge to provide three to five recommended candidates to the chief executive officer (CEO), the group should not deliver one or two candidates or more than five candidates. Even with a formal charge, there may be *implied provisions* of the mission. Implied provisions are elements that are never stated by the superior, per se, but which the superior assumes will be part of the consideration of the group. For example, if the organization and the CEO have taken a strong affirmative action position, the group should include women and minorities in its 3-5 recommended candidates.

Group and Individual Agendas

The goal of the group may be *new*, as in the case of hiring a new person. The goal may be *rebuilt* as in the case of developing a revised marketing plan for a product that is already being produced and sold. The goal may be a matter of *maintenance*, such as developing a means for maintaining the sales and profit levels. The goal may be *ongoing* as in creating ways to keep the image of the organization at a high level (Smith, 1965). But in any case, the goal always has a barrier or barriers.

"A barrier is any circumstance or force that prevents an individual or group from attaining a stated goal" (Smith, 1965, p. 25). For example, a barrier to hiring a new person may be that there are not enough candidates to present 3-5 acceptable ones. A new marketing plan may be too expensive to initialize. Sales and profit levels may be so high that increasing them is virtually impossible. How to maintain one's image may be too abstract to make concrete. All of those barriers are part of the original charge.

However, barriers are also created by individual members of the group. The most effective groups have agreement about the charge and the barriers to achieving the charge. When all agree, this is called a *common goal*. Unfortunately, individual egos often surface while the group is in process. For example, some members of the group may think that the CEO has already made a decision, in which case such members believe they are there simply to "pre-rubber stamp" the decision. In other cases, the members of the group may have their own biases about candidates for a position. Some may oppose the affirmative action principles while others are adamant about affirmative action. Some group members may want to make decisions as quickly as possible, while others may think that the group process should work itself out over a period of time.

Individual agendas, goals for the group which are unstated and not part of the charge, can be highly detrimental to the effective working of a meeting. The chair may view the group work as his or her opportunity to "get ahead" in the organization, thereby focusing on what the CEO wants more so than on what the organization needs. Other members may feel that group meetings are a waste of time, especially since they need the time to undertake tasks which they feel are more important.

Early in the meeting, it is important for the new member to analyze the "motives" or agendas of each of the other parties in the group. In addition to what is said in the meeting, the new group member must keep abreast of such agendas through what is known as the *informal communication network* or the grapevine. The grapevine is the talk that takes place outside of the formal meetings of the group. A member may come into the office of the new group member and suggest that such-and-such a decision should or should not be made at the next meeting.

We know (Goldhaber, 1993) that the informal communication network has at least four characteristics:

1. *The grapevine is fast.*
2. *The grapevine is accurate.*
3. *The grapevine carries much information.*
4. *The grapevine travels by cluster.*

When other members of the organization are aware of a meeting and a group, information about it travels fast. This is especially the case when the final recommendations may be negative for other members of the organization (for example, the elimination of "flex-time"; downsizing in the organization; the closing of offices; etc.). The people within the group and outside the group know more information than CEOs expect them to know. Those outside the group often characterize the reasons why certain people were appointed to the group. The information is usually "connected" to other information in the organization.

Rules, Roles, and Routines

All organizations function through the use of rules, roles, and routines. As a new member of a group, it is critical to determine what each of one them involves. This is especially true if the group previously existed. *Rules* are the norms of the group; they are what is expected. For example, is it acceptable to show up for a meeting late? Who should be notified if you will be absent from a group meeting? Is it acceptable to leave early? If so, for what reason? How long do the meetings last? *Roles* are positions that group members typically take. These will be discussed in a later section of this chapter. *Routines* involve participation in meetings. As a new member, should you feel like you can speak out? Who really makes the decisions in the group? Is there a pattern about where each member sits?

In anticipation of the meeting, the new member should consider the charge of the group. Such consideration should be based upon the ambiguity of the charge, the formality of the charge, as well as diversity of opinion about the charge. You should be aware of the various agendas involved which may or may not be relevant to the charge. Finally, the new member should gain an impression early in the first meeting of the rules, roles, and routines which are part of the group culture.

Encounter

The first meeting has begun. The chair of the group has provided the charge. The members are seated in their preferred places, and as a new member, you have taken the position that remains. As you begin analyzing the problem outlined in the charge, you will also begin analyzing the *meeting process*. If you have not met each other person in the group, you will be introduced. Often members of a group will introduce themselves, telling a little about their jobs.

While many believe this is a relatively unimportant part of the group process, it may help you in the further analysis of roles, rules, and routines. Exactly what each person says about himself/herself may help you to learn to characterize the others in the group. William S. Smith (1965, pp. 192-195) has provided a list of 14 possible roles that people play in the group meeting process. As we discuss these, we should remember that we should refrain from stereotyping individuals as *unidimensional*—thinking and acting the same way under all circumstances. We should also realize that each individual may play more than one role in meetings and several individuals may play the same role. Just as a note on "playing a role": we do not intend to infer that the people were pretending, although some may be. Playing a role is much like taking a position. In this case, the position may not be about the task at hand, the charge, so much as it is where one fits into the group. We will discuss each of the 14 roles and then analyze what they mean altogether.

Roles of Group Members

The eager beaver. This person may be described as anxious about going about the task. The reasons or motives for such eagerness may vary from person to person. If the individual believes that the group task is unimportant, she may want to move through the process quickly. If the person is *task-oriented*, he may want to quickly complete it. A task-oriented individual is one who is generally less able to engage in small talk, one who thinks that work is work, and play is play. The eager beaver is likely to be a list-maker, highly organized, efficient. This person does not like any moving away from the topic at hand. "There is a job to do, let's roll up our sleeves and do it," may be the motto of the eager beaver.

The talker. This individual may also be anxious. He may be verbose, using too many words to state his position. On many occasions, his talk will not be relevant to the charge or to the task at hand. He often talks in a manner which indicates that he hasn't had a chance to talk much elsewhere and may never have a chance to talk again. He is typically unable to read the nonverbal signals of others in the group who may want to interrupt or move on. The talker's motto may be: "I need to get out all that I want to say because I may never have another chance."

The brilliant one. This person's role may or may not be associated with her intelligence quotient. The fact is, though, that she and others *believe* she's smart. Her ideas may be more impractical. She is concerned that what she says *sounds* smart. She may not say very much, but others listen to her carefully. She may be less sensitive to the ideas of others because she believes that their ideas are less worthwhile. The motto of the brilliant one is: "I want to say something for which the others will remember is a super idea."

The emotional one. This person is involved and aroused by the group process. His emotions may be based on the charge itself or even something totally unrelated to the topic. He takes the proceedings very seriously. He may speak loudly, sometimes even inappropriately using curse words. He is easily upset by what he may consider undue repetition, which he perceives as slowing the group down.

His voice may break at times because of his feelings about what he is saying. He may be seated somewhat away from the discussion table. His motto is: "This process is very serious to *me, my feelings* are at stake here."

The bored one. Typically this person does not like meetings at all. She feels that decisions can be better made in some other fashion. She finds the members of the group and/or the charge useless. Her nonverbal behavior emphasizes her disinterest in what is going on. Rarely, if ever, will she be impressed with anything that someone else says. She will probably talk very little. Her motto is: "Let's get this garbage over with."

The silent one. This person is a low-level participant. He probably says little because he doesn't especially like to talk in groups and/or feels that he has nothing to say about the charge. When he does have an idea, he feels that he can wait for someone else to say it, for if it is important someone else will take the reins. When he does speak, the others listen more carefully because of his erstwhile silence. He is often a good listener to what the others are saying, though he is unlikely to comment of their positions. He probably dislikes conflict in the group. He is in no real hurry as long as he is not asked to participate very much. His motto is: "I'll sit here and listen and wait for the process and the decision to be complete."

The conformist. She will go along with whatever the others say and do. She tends to avoid disagreement. She thinks that others will like her so long as she does not alienate anyone. Her comments will be reinforcing of comments made by others. "I think that's a good idea." She does not like conflict because that makes her feel forced to choose between or among opposing ideas. She is not a position taker. She might engage in a conversation like this. "What do you think?" may be asked of her. Her answer may be, "I don't know, what do the rest of you think?" Her motto is: "Do unto others, and maybe they will do unto you."

The recognition-seeker. For the recognition seeker, the group meeting is another chance to play politics and receive applause. He may be the first to speak. He wants to ensure that the final results come from his ideas and that all of the group members recall that it was his ideas that brought success to the group. The recognition-seeker is *not* a good team or group player. He wants credit. He expects the others to listen to him and quote him later. The motto of the recognition-seeker is: "Let's all agree that I made the group a success."

The playboy/playgirl. This is an individual who is trying to impress at least one group member of the opposite sex. At times, the flirtation may be sincere. At other times, the flirtation is merely a game which has been learned. Stroking of the hair, primping, appealing to sensuous urges of others are behaviors typifying the playboy/playgirl. He or she may be more interested in gaining a mate from work than in keeping one's job. Sometimes colleagues who are seeing one another outside of work both play these roles with one another in group meetings. The motto is: "Let's quit work and go play."

The suspicious one. This person is concerned about motives of everyone in the group. To some extent, this individual is mildly paranoid. For example, when the charge is given, the suspicious one doubts whether the stated charge is the *real* charge. He may wonder why he was placed in the group and why other members were placed in the group. He doubts the sincerity of the others in the group. He believes there is always an underlying motive. Both the content (charge) and the group process are under suspicion. His motto is: "Why are we *really* here?"

The non-conformist. To some extent, the non-conformist will disagree simply to disagree. This person may or may not dress differently from others. She does think, though, that her ideas should be unusual, unlike those of the other group members. She will often sit away from others in the group, to illustrate her non-conformity. She will rarely, if ever, be the chair of the group because others in the organization are aware of her position. More often than not, however, she is placed in the group to provide an element of creativity and/or argumentation that may be absent from the group when she is not there. She is probably less concerned about the rules and routines than are other group members. Her motto is: "I'm way out here, distancing myself away from you."

The aggressive one. This one is assertive to put it mildly. He may be loud. He certainly makes himself noticed. He is the virtual opposite of the silent one. He may or may not talk a great deal, but he will ensure that he is heard. His ideas may be supportive of others in the group or his ideas may be of a non-conformist nature. He will get in his "two cents worth." Other members of the group have a tendency to support his ideas, even though they may not have thought them out well. He is capable of driving the group to a bad decision, but is just as capable of driving it toward a good decision. The important word here is "drive." His motto is: "You *must* listen to what I have to say." Typically, he is not a very good listener.

The debunker. She believes that she has nothing to contribute and neither does anyone else in the group. Her role is to "knock ideas down." She is constantly trying to finds reasons and ways of showing that something will not work. "It is too expensive. It will take too long. We tried it before, and it didn't work then." While ideas may well get through the group, she will undertake every method possible to see that they don't. Other members of the group find the debunker to be a frustrating person with whom to work. Her motto is: "It just won't work."

The special pleader. This group member is characterized much like a child whiner. He may be pleading to "hurry up and move on." He may be pleading for his ideas or for the ideas of someone else in the group. He may plead for the group to get back on the track. He may plead for obtaining more data before making a decision. His motto is: "Please, please, please, please."

The politician. This individual is trying to resolve any conflicts in the group by trying to appease both sides. He wants the group to be a success. He smiles a lot. He gives credit to others. He may or may not have ideas of his own, although more often than not he doesn't because this might cause some conflict in the group. He tries to bring together the charge and the CEOs' ideas with the ideas of those in the group. He sounds like a politician on the campaign trail. Whereas the debunker sees no good in ideas, the politician sees only good in the ideas. Anything may work. His motto is: "We can work this all out for the benefit of everyone."

The blocker. The primary objective of the blocker is to see to it that the goal is never accomplished. The most typical strategy of the blocker is to postpone, delay, find alternative reasons why the group cannot move on. She is insistent in trying to maintain the status quo, which may be threatened should the group accomplish its mission. Unlike the debunker, she may not disagree about everything. Instead she utilizes a process of delay. The blocker is usually in the center of the talkers because her viewpoint must be represented. Her motto is: "Put off today what can be done tomorrow."

The model member. The model member is the kind of group participant that each group should wish to have. There is no self-aggrandizement on the part of the model member. He or she is not trying to accomplish feats for himself but for the group. He or she participates. He carefully listens to others. She analyzes before critiquing. He tries to get silent members to participate. She is concerned about group outcomes.

In short, then, the roles of group members vary according to their ego-involvement in the process. They vary in accordance with listening and talking preferences. They vary in terms of emphasis on the quality of group decisions and the amount of time devoted to achieving a proper decision. They vary to the extent to which they are interested in the group itself. Finally, they vary to the extent that they are task-oriented or socially-oriented. Understanding roles and group orientation are important elements of the socialization process. Once the new member understands these factors, she is ready to look at rules and routines.

Task and Social Orientation

When individuals interact in conversation or in group meetings, they tend to vary to the extent that they are interested in task and social orientation. Many everyday conversations are strictly socially oriented. A *social orientation* is when the individuals talking are trying to get to know one another as human beings. People talk about their families, their hobbies, and their interests. There is no task-at-hand. A social orientation is for the purpose of getting to know one another better.

A *task orientation* is when the group or individuals are "talking business." When discussion is oriented toward the task, there is less concern about the personal aspects of the people involved. For example, when you are on vacation and you stop to ask for directions, your concern is with how to get to your destination. You are not really concerned about the family of the person who is providing directions.

In meetings, time is usually spent on social maintenance aspects as well as task aspects. Because the members of the group may see one another only at meetings, a certain amount of time is spent "catching up" with one another. Developing the *social orientation* is as important for the group as is the task orientation because social elements help meld the group together. Members tend to work together better when they know each other. It is important to remember that each group member has relationships outside the group. Such relationships are known as *linkages*.

Linkages

There are two types of linkages that group members possess. There are *formal networks*, which are composed of those they know at work through the official chain of command. When one is entering a new group, an important part of the socialization process is determining these relationships. Which of the members is closest to the CEO? Which members have authority over other members of the group? There are also *informal networks* or linkages. For example, some members may play golf with one another. They may have children in the same school. Both the formal and informal networks operate in three different ways.

Downward communication occurs when a superior hands down information to a subordinate. This is what takes place when the group is given its charge. These types of information include job instructions, job rationale, procedures and practice, feedback on job performance, and the indoctrination of goals. *Upward communication* goes in the opposite direction. This includes the final report that the group returns to the superior. Questions and suggestions are part of this upward communication spiral. *Horizontal communication* takes place between individuals of similar status. It is best when the members of the group are of similar status. Of course, the chair of the committee may often be superior to the other members of the group.

Knowing the nature of roles and group orientation provides the newcomer an opportunity for becoming acquainted with the personality of the group. Of course, she should also analyze the relationships of each member within the group. At times, votes will be taken either in a formal manner or an informal manner. The outcome of such decisions should be known before the decision is actually made. From this information, the member can go on to determine the rules and routines of the group.

Rules and Routines of the Group

Group rules are expected behaviors. There are expected behaviors about what time one should arrive and what time one should leave. In addition, there are rules about what words to say in a meeting. Sometimes there are rules about how long the meetings will last. Incidental events are also connected to the behavior of people in groups. For example, should a secretary interrupt the proceedings of the group for *any* reason? Should individuals take telephone calls during the meeting? Should substitutes be sent to a meeting when a member cannot be there? Most of these facets of group meetings are never openly discussed, but there are implicit rules about them. What should one wear to a meeting? Should you take something to take notes on or will paper be provided? Will there be a written formal agenda at each meeting? Will the agenda be available in advance of the meeting? Are members allowed to add items to the agenda?

The best way for new group members to determine answers to each of these questions is to observe carefully what goes on. Such issues as a person talking too little or too much may be approved or disapproved only by slight facial expressions of some members. The new member must be sensitive to such expressions as well as checking the behavior of others about the expression. The new member needs to learn which other members' opinions count and which seem not to count. A continual monitoring of the situation is essential to analyze the power balance within the group.

Identification

Identification occurs when the new member feels part of the group. For some new members, this may occur after only two or three meetings. For others, this process may take a very long time. For example, when members resent a new member because she was hired in a competition with one of the other members, it may take months or longer to be accepted. The first phase of identification is **compliance**. Here the new member acts in accordance with the expectations of the other members. These expectations may be a combination of the group's anticipation of the individual as well as whatever role or roles the individual has taken on. Second, the individual must identify with the **values** of the group. Finally, your own values and those of the group are melded together so that they appear inseparable. It is important to note that the individual must attempt to maintain his individuality, but this is relatively difficult once such values have been inculcated into the new personality. Nevertheless, group members must avoid a tendency of "groupthink," a situation in which all members tend to think alike regardless of the situation.

Summary

New members undergo an initiation process into the group. To be successful in the group, the new member must go through three phases. First is the anticipation stage. Many have difficulty with this stage because they think that the new group will function the same way as the last group with which they worked. However, it is important for the new member to analyze the roles, rules, and routines of group members to establish his/her own *modus operandi*. Once group work begins, more intense analysis of the group is necessary. In this encounter stage, the member interacts with the others, analyzing not only the content of the charge and its ultimate outcome but also the processes of group work itself.

With some knowledge of how we enter and progress through the workings of a group, we will next focus on developing purposeful meetings. Perhaps the first question that should be asked about any meeting is: "Do we *really* need to have a meeting about this?" Chapter Three will provide some answers to when groups need to meet as well as discuss a number of different reasons one may not want to call a meeting.

References

Barge, J. K., & Schlueter, D. W. (2004). Memorable messages and newcomer socialization. *Western Journal of Communication, 68,* 233-256.

Conrad, C. (1994). *Strategic organizational communication: Toward the twenty-first century.* Fort Worth, TX: Harcourt Brace.

Goldhaber, G. (1993). *Organizational communication* (6th ed.). Madison, WI: Brown & Benchmark.

Hickson, M. III, & Stacks, D. W. (1998). *Organizational communication in the personal context: From interview to retirement.* Boston: Allyn and Bacon.

Smith, W. S. (1965). *Group problem-solving through discussion: A process essential to democracy.* Indianapolis: Bobbs-Merrill

1. Joining a New Group

Assume that you've just joined a new civic organization. What factors should you consider when trying to understand the norms of the group? How will you go about identifying those norms? Remember that you have fewer "credits" with the group than do experienced members. That means that you must take extra steps, following a safety first rule. Under that principle, why should you . . .

Never use profanity or tell offensive jokes, even if other members do?
Arrive early for group meetings?
Dress conservatively?
Ask a lot of questions?

2. Your First Day on a New Job

You've just graduated from college, had your interview, and now you're getting ready to join an important new group—your first job. What things should you consider and do so that (1) you'll fit in, (2) be a positive force within the organization, and (3) increase your chances for advancement? Consider each of the following points and how they may influence (good or bad) your socialization process within this work organization.

A. Consider the importance of time. What time will you arrive for work? When will you leave? What about the recommendation that you should be the first to arrive and the last to leave, at least for a while?

B. How will you dress? Do you understand the dress code of the organization? Is there a difference between the way entry level and upper level personnel dress?

C. Will you have a lot of questions to ask of others? You should generally listen more than you talk, with much of your own "talking" falling into the category of questions.

D. The "listen more than you talk" rule should be followed to the extreme when it comes to the office "grapevine." A new employee can learn a lot about an organization by listening to office rumors, but that same rookie should not be contributing to that grapevine. Listen to what's going on, but don't contribute to the rumors.

E. Don't forget to smile. Your first day on the job will have a major impact on the first impression of you that your co-workers will have. What can you do to make that first impression a positive one?

3. Comparing Civic Groups to the Work Place

Earlier you were asked to discuss how you might ingratiate yourself into a civic organization and into a work-place organizations. How were the two situations similar? How were they different? Would the same principles apply to social or service groups? Do you think these principles would work for meeting your new parents-in-law?

CHAPTER 3

INTERPERSONAL DYNAMICS IN GROUPS

Group problem solving and decision making is complicated by the interpersonal dynamics of groups and their members. No group is an entity unto itself. Instead, groups are composed of individual members who enter the group process with individual goals, individual agendas, and individual motives. This is further complicated by individual variations in communication skills, status, and commitment to the group goal. Some of the specific individual factors which influence group activity the most are (1) power, (2) conflict and (3) interpersonal relationships.

Power

Power is discussed in more detail in Chapter 9 ("Leadership"). The discussion here will be limited to the role of power in interpersonal dynamics. Heilbrun (1988) defined power as the ability to take one's place in whatever discourse is essential to action and the right to have one's part matter. Korda (1975) defined sense of power as "a gut-feel of being able to predict with some degree of certainty how people will react in certain situations, so you can predict when there is going to be trouble over something" (p. 44). In terms of group processes, power can be considered the capacity to influence one's circumstances and the outcomes of the group.

A common misconception of power is that it is a quality that an individual has within the group setting. Actually, power is a relational property of the group environment, not a trait that applies to an individual. An individual has power within a group to the extent that others believe they have such power. Those other individuals are dependent upon the power person (1) to the extent that they believe the power figure can have influence on outcomes which affect their circumstances, and (2) the extent to which other avenues to reach that outcome are available.

Participants in an organizational conflict enter the arena with a variety of power agents at their disposal. The effective use of power depends on the extent that an individual's **power currencies** are what other people need, and the extent to which that individual can use the power currencies under their control. Some parties may dominate in some areas, while others might dominate in others.

The Components of Power

While many factors can influence the overall effectiveness of power, three particular factors—control, concern, and scrutiny—seem to have an impact on probable compliance. Followers are more likely to comply with a request if they believe the power source (1) controls the power they are attempting to use, (2) considers the request to be important, and (3) will verify whether or not the order has been carried out.

Control. The ability of any individual to have power over another person is based partly upon the perceived control which they have over their power source. If an individual relies upon reward power as the basis of their leadership, for example, then the followers must believe that the leader has the ability to provide those rewards. A supervisor may promise a promotion to someone if they successfully complete a project, but that power play will only be effective if the target of the instruction believes that particular supervisor is capable of fulfilling that promise. If they believe that someone else in the department has decisional power over promotions, then perceived control decreases and the likelihood of compliance decreases. Similarly, another supervisor may use coercive power, threatening to fire anyone who disobeys her. However, if the people under her believe that those decisions are made by someone higher in the organization, then they are less likely to feel threatened by the attempted use of coercive power.

Concern. Compliance with a power request increases in situations reflecting high concern. Followers of a person with power are more likely to comply with his request if they believe that the person considers the request an important one. If they believe the power source is joking, or that they are making a request only to meet the minimum requirement of some rule, then there will be less likely to obey the request.

Scrutiny. Scrutiny refers to the perception among the followers as to whether or not the power source will check or verify that the order has been followed. If they believe verification will occur, compliance is more easily obtained. If they believe there will be no scrutiny or verification, then compliance is likely to slip.

Power and Credibility

Many beginning students of group processes confuse the terms power and credibility. This happens frequently because (1) both terms refer to the ability of a person to influence others, and (2) there are some obvious similarities between some components of power and some elements of credibility. There is still a crucial difference between power and credibility, though. *Power is focused on gaining compliance, or behavioral change; credibility aims at influencing attitudes.* Further, the impact of credibility is a long term one which can influence attitudes and behavior over time. Power tends to focus on gaining compliant behavior in a specific situation.

Impact of Power

The presence of power affects group participants in a variety of ways. One common occurrence is the presence of ***power denial***. Individuals may assert that they have no power, or deny that they tried to use power in any manner. This is most frequently exhibited by members who deny that they said something or that they were attempting to use power in any manner.

The presence of power within the group inevitably leads to the development of power imbalances, sometimes with negative effects. A group member who consistently maintains a high power position may acquire a taste for power, with the attainment of power becoming an end into itself. High power members may also devalue the worth of the less powerful members, leading to reduced social contact. That may lead to the other members giving them false feedback and reducing the effectiveness of the group.

If the other groups members consistently see themselves in a low power position, their self esteem within the group is diminished and their communication tactics tend to change. Sometimes rebellion emerges in the form of aggression, violence or dirty tactics. At other times, they may simply give up and stop contributing to the group. Either way, the productivity of the group is diminished.

People who have learned to use power productively have learned the value of restraint, or what might be called the **Power of Calm Persistence**. They limit their power by refusing to use currencies at their disposal, focusing on the interdependence of the groups rather than their needs as a power source. And, rather than trying to attain more power, they distribute some of that power to low power members.

Conflict

Conflict will be discussed more thoroughly in Chapter 6, but some understanding of the concept is essential to understanding the interpersonal dynamics of a group. The issue starts with individual group members and their attitudes toward conflict.

Is conflict within a group a good thing or a bad thing? How you answer that will depend upon your own personal view of conflict in group situations. Some people have a positive opinion toward conflict. For them, conflict encourages open discussion of ideas, stirs up creative ways of looking at a problem, and represents truth and democracy in its ultimate form. When conflict is not allowed, ideas are stifled and freedom of expression is inhibited.

Others view conflict negatively. For them, conflict is indicative of group processes which have gone awry, tempers which have lost control, and discussions which have degenerated into negative comments. Conflict leads to hurt feelings rather than discussion of ideas. Pragmatically, though, work and social groups should view conflict as an inevitable part of the process. It will occur. The only question in doubt is how the group members will handle any conflict that might arise. Depending upon their background, each member might view conflict from a number of different perspectives. These might include:

- **No big deal.** For some people, conflict is not a major problem. They view it as a normal process which occurs when problems need to be solved.
- **Cooperation.** Conflict might be viewed as a positive stimulus against an outside threat, serving as impetus for cooperation as the parties unite against a common foe.

- **Expectations of constant tension.** For some, particularly those who grow up in an openly hostile environment, conflict conjures up expectations of constant tension—the fear that any event can set off a fire storm.

- **Chaos.** Some people view conflict as being synonymous with chaos. For them, conflict is not a disagreement over ideas so much as a destruction of process.

- **Communication breakdown.** Many people view conflict merely as a breakdown in communication. It may be a breakdown in the entire process, in which chaos occurs. Or it may be a simple breakdown in the transfer of meaning which translates into hurt feelings and misunderstandings. In fact, many conflict situations are caused by communication breakdowns, but the two terms are not synonymous. Actually, communication between the two parties can be highly effective and still be high in conflict, if there is basic disagreement over their ideas.

Types of Conflict

Whether conflict is positive or negative can sometimes depend upon the type of conflict involved. Consider these variations of situations, and the range of conflict which they reflect.

1. *Humorous conflict.* Our society often uses humor as a means of invoking mild forms of conflict. Sometimes humor is used for positive reasons, to increase interpersonal cohesiveness. Others times, it has a negative intent, used as an underhanded swipe to throw a blow at an opponent.

Wilmot and Hocker (2000) describe one positive form of humorous conflict as *mock conflict*. Mock conflict has a playful intent and is used by some people to increase cohesiveness and maintain relationships. In movies, mock conflict is a basic form of interaction in "buddy" films, with two men constantly kidding each other. Movies which have used mock conflict include the classic western film, *Butch Cassidy and the Sundance Kid* and the more current comedies such as *Grumpy Old Men* and the *Rush Hour* series.

A more serious form of humorous conflict is *sarcasm*. Sarcasm involves the use of humor to make hostile remarks about another person. When this is done in a mild manner, it may fall within the realm of mock conflict. When the remark becomes too harsh, however, it crosses into the realm of sniping and can result in damage to a relationship.

2. *Silent Conflict*. Sometimes conflict is not verbalized at all, at least not to the person who is the target of the conflict behavior. The most common form of silent conflict is the *silent treatment* in which one person refuses to talk to another across two or more interactions. The person engaging in the silent treatment views it as (1) expressing displeasure toward the other person, and (2) providing the other person with a form of aversive stimulation.

Another form of silent conflict is *indirect conflict*. In indirect conflict, a person's never speaks of their conflict with the person who made them angry, but they engage in other behaviors which provide them with a means of revenge. Such conflict often surfaces in business organizations when an employee feels they have been mistreated by management but that they either lack a means of expressing their feelings or they fear they might be punished if they express their feelings. Instead of taking their complaint to a supervisor, they retaliate by sabotaging some aspect of the supervisor's program. In extreme forms, indirect conflict may be a person's justification for stealing or embezzling from an employer.

3. *Discussions of issues*. A positive form of conflict is a discussion of issues between two parties. In its most positive form, the discussion focuses on the question under consideration, rather than the individuals involved.

4. *Repetitive conflicts*. One negative form of conflict which surfaces in some long-term relationships is that of repetitive conflicts. Repetitive conflicts tend to fall into two subcategories. *Deja vu conflict* is the term used to describe a series of serious conflicts which have a predictable pattern of repetition. Once something triggers such a conflict, the parties involved tend to repeat arguments and statements which they have used in previous arguments. Once these are exhausted, the conflict may die down, but no resolution is reached. Instead, the disagreement lies dormant until something else triggers it again. When that happens, as Yogi Berra once said, "It's *deja vu* all over again."

Sometimes repetitive conflicts get increasingly more hostile, leading to an *escalatory spiral*. As each side articulates its argument, animosity from the opponent increases. That, in turn, increases animosity from the first party. As the cycle repeats, the tensions increase and the conflict worsens. Such a spiral can occur over the duration of many conflict incidents, or it may occur within a single conflict episode.

5. *Blow-ups.* Blow-ups are heated emotional exchanges with strong expressions of hostility. Sometimes blow-ups are the culmination of an escalatory spiral, with the growing tensions mounting to the point that conflict reaches an explosive level. On other occasions, blow-ups may be the by-product of a series of small conflicts or perceptions of injustices. Such surprise blow-ups are particularly common in high-stress environments. In a moderate form, surprise blow-ups may take the form of an otherwise calm employee who suddenly starts yelling at co-workers and/or customers. In a more serious form, it can be deadly, with the individual killing or wounding people they deem responsible for the injustices down against them.

Clarify and Verify
There are no easy answers for managing conflict within groups, but each member can engage in two activities which can make group conflict more productive: (1) clarify you messages and (2) verify your perceptions.

Clarify your messages. Sometimes, the source of the conflict is an inaccurate perception of something you, as a member, might have said. In those instances, it is crucial that the other group members have an accurate assessment of what you mean. That requires that you describe both what you mean and how you feel about an issue. Summarize your opinion rationally, without attacking the other participant(s).

Check your perceptions. Your perceptions often have a stronger impact on conflict than does reality. For that reason, you must ascertain that your perceptions of the situation are accurate. Express your perceptions to others, ask direct questions about what is happening, and listen closely to the replies.

Individual Relational Factors
Group members enter the group with both personal and group histories which can influence how other group members will respond to them. For a number of reasons, they may be better liked, more believable, and easier to get along with than some of the other participants. Generally, the factors which most frequently influence this individual relationships within the group are (1) similarity, (2) interpersonal attractiveness, and (3) interpersonal credibility.

Similarity or Homophily
When meeting another person for the first time, one of the first evaluations which we make is whether or not that person is "like us."

If they are viewed as "one of us," then most other evaluations which follow are positive ones. If not, the first impression is likely to be a negative one. Such a negative reaction could be caused by any one of several dimensions of similarity.

Attitudinal Similarity. Attitudinal similarity is the extent to which we believe another person's attitude's are similar to our own. This is a "thinks like me" evaluation, and it has its most obvious embodiment in clubs and organizations with similar attitudinal goals—political parties, special interest organizations, and professional organizations.

Value Similarity. Value similarity has close parallels to attitudinal similarity, except that the similarities go to deeper perceptions of morality and views about right and wrong. This form of similarity has the most potential to bring people together. If another person is considered to be someone who "shares my values," then the chances of a long-term relationship are higher. This form of similarity tends to be strong among religious groups, for example, and it is particularly strong within religious cults.

Physical Similarity. Physical similarity is the extent to which we believe another person's physical appearance is similar to our own, a "looks like me" response. People quite frequently associate with others who share common physical characteristics, including such obvious variables as height and weight.

Social Similarity. Social similarity is the extent to which we believe a person comes from the same social background as ourselves. Generally, most people feel more comfortable around people of their own social class. People from a higher social class are viewed as snobs who "put on airs." People from a lower social class "have no class."

Compensations for Differences

While similarity increases the chances for positive relationship, the presence of differences does not mean that relationships are doomed to failure. Instead, the barriers created by those differences can be overcome by techniques which compensate for this, a process called *compensations for heterophily.*

Frequent interactions can compensate for many of these differences. As you increasingly communicate with another person, you will get to know them better, they get to know you, and more areas of similarity may be found. Further, even if differences still dominate the relationship, it will be easier to understand the source of the differences.

The *development of empathy* is another factor which can compensate for personal differences. Although we make quick judgments about attitudinal homophily, it is not an over-riding requirement for friendship. Friends don't have to agree on everything, but they do need to understand each other. The development of empathy, then, can become more important than similarity. *Feedback* is the major means of achieving empathy. By providing each other with feedback regarding the accuracy or inaccuracy of impressions, then perceived differences can be reduced and understanding can be increased.

Interpersonal Attraction

Interpersonal attraction is a measure of how attracted one person is toward another. It serves as the stimulus for interpersonal relationships for both work situations and informal social environments. Rather than being a one-dimensional concept, however, it is really composed of at least three separate components.

Types of Interpersonal Attraction

Task Attraction. Task attraction is the extent to which one person is attracted to another as a potential co-worker. Is the other person someone with whom you would enjoy working? Would working with them likely be a pleasant work environment? Are they someone who would make you and your co-workers more productive, or would they increase the strain of producing within your work environment?

Social Attraction. Social attraction is the extent to which one person is attracted to another in terms of social situations. Is the other person someone who might make a good friend? Are they someone with whom you could enjoy doing things in social situation? Would you enjoy having lunch together, shopping together, or spending time together away from the office?

Physical Attraction. Physical attractiveness is the evaluation which one person makes about another's physical appearance. If the person is a male, would they be considered handsome or good-looking? For females, are they pretty, cute, or gorgeous? To what extent do they approach these descriptions? Physical attractiveness is particularly important in cross-gender, male-female interactions. Its role also tends to be more influential among unmarried individuals, but it can impact overall interpersonal attractiveness. It can also effect other components of interpersonal attraction. For example, people who are excessively overweight are often viewed as physically unattractive by many people, and this rating may also cause them to be rated low on either social attraction, task attraction, or both.

Factors Affecting Interpersonal Attraction

A number of factors have an impact on how we evaluate other people in terms of interpersonal attraction. One of the most important is *gender.* Generally, males tend focus on task attractiveness when they evaluate other people, particularly other males. The primary concern of males, in many cases, is how the person would be as a potential co-worker. Women tend to focus on social attraction, particularly in terms of other women. Their primary concern is how friendly the person seems to be.

Another factor which influences interpersonal attraction is *homophily*, or similarity. We tend to find people more attractive if we think they have many things in common with ourselves. Similarity is particularly important for the dimension of physical attractiveness. We tend to have the strongest physical attraction toward members of the opposite sex whom we evaluate as being similar to ourselves, but slightly more attractive than how we evaluate ourselves. A person whom we evaluate as considerably less attractive than oneself is considered undesirable; someone who is considerably more attractive than oneself is considered unapproachable. It is not uncommon for beauty queens, for example, to have trouble finding dates, because the males in their social circles assume they are not attractive enough for them.

Credibility

Credibility is one of the oldest concepts in the development of communication theory. It appears in the rhetorical theory of the ancient Greeks, discussed by Aristotle as the concept of *ethos*. Latin scholars had a similar appreciation for the idea. Quintilian, for example, argued that the essence of persuasion was the idea of "a good man speaking well." In modern communication theory, that concept has been expanded into a number of subcategories. Each of these can contribute, in varying degrees, to the credibility of a person within an organization.

Character. In most instances, the factor which has the biggest impact upon a person's overall credibility is their character. This refers to the evaluation that others make about the moral character of the individual. It is often articulated by other group members with terms such as integrity or honesty.

Competence. Competence, or capability, is generally the second most important factor in a person's credibility. This refers to others evaluation of a person's credibility, at least in terms of how it applies to the issue or job at hand. In most situations, the factors of character and competence account for two-thirds or more of a person's total credibility rating. Still, some other variables can influence that overall image, including the following.

Composure. Composure refers to the perceived ability of a person to remain calm under pressure. During a crisis, or in other high-stress situations, composure can become an important factor in influencing subordinate impressions of a leader's credibility.

Sociability. Sociability refers to the perceived friendliness of a person. In many situations, it ranks third in importance (behind only character and competence) in influencing judgments from co-workers. People are more likely to believe someone who treats them in a friendly manner. Because of this, a number of illegal con games are based upon this factor, with one person taking advantage of another by engaging in dubious activities while acting in a friendly manner.

Extroversion. Extroversion, or verbosity, refers to the talkativeness or outgoing personality of an individual. It can have both a positive and negative impact on overall credibility. On the positive side, some degree of extroversion increases credibility. The ability to articulate ideas to others is a positive factor which increases competence ratings, thus increasing overall credibility. On the negative side, excessive verbosity is viewed as a negative within our culture. The person can be perceived as a show-off, or an "all-talk-and-no-action" individual. External factors which increase extroversion perceptions can also affect other dimensions of an individual's credibility. Hickson, et al (1988), for example, found that cigar smokers tended to receive higher ratings on extroversion that non-smokers or cigarette smokers, but there was also a corresponding drop in their perceived intelligence.

The Extended Inference

One amazing aspect of all three dimensions of personal image—similarity, interpersonal attraction, and credibility—is that we tend to make these evaluations of others very quickly. For that reason, first impressions tend to be extremely important in forming long-term relationship. There is an element of self-recognition in the process, in that we realize our first impression may be wrong. For that reason, we tend to be flexible in our evaluations as we get to know a person, making adjustments as we get to know them better. Still, that first impression can influence even those long-term evaluations. A similarity evaluation is made quickly, for example, often within the first few seconds of meeting another person. Perceived similarity, in turn, often serves as a base for evaluating another person's character. In essence, if a person is considered "different from us," we may not trust them.

The process for such extended inferences tends to vary among males and females. Males, in particular, are concerned about similarity, particularly in terms of shared attitudes; they may delay any definitive evaluations about the other person's character. Women, though, tend to focus more quickly on situational concerns (social attraction) and credibility evaluations.

The Saboteur

Often work groups find themselves with an unmotivated member, someone whose lack of enthusiasm interferes with the ability of the group to achieve its goal. Such group members become *saboteurs*, participants who ultimately may undermine the group and its goals. Saboteurs can develop within a group whenever there is a significant difference between group goals and individual goals. Frequently the sabotage is unintentional on the part of the saboteur in that they do not deliberately interfering with group goals. Still, a failure on their part to complete assigned tasks can effectively disrupt group achievements.

Even the suspicion of sabotage can undermine group efforts (Thompson & Pearce, 1992). If sabotage is suspected, group members tend to lose sight of the group goal, and all communication becomes focused on the potential sabotage. The group is unlikely to return to productive work until the matter has been resolved, often by either a direct or indirect ostracizing of the suspected saboteur.

In such cases, the ostracized member will frequently realize what has happened. Further, they can frequently explain why, although from an individualized viewpoint. A typical explanation from the ostracized member is, "They probably didn't think I was contributing enough, because my work schedule kept me from attending a lot of the meetings." That statement recognizes the reason for the ostracizing (lack of contribution) and the behavioral pattern that spurred the ostracizing (skipping meetings), but provides a benign motive for the behavior (schedule conflicts). Other group members are likely to view this explanation with skepticism. Even if the explanation is correct, many of the other members will assume they have made sacrifices in their schedule to accommodate group activities, and they will expect other members to do the same.

Another form of sabotage, **backstabbing**, is sabotage which is directed at specific group member instead of toward the group as a whole. Dilenschneider (1997) noted that the best way to counter backstabbing is to have other allies within the group who will tell you what is going on and who will help you to stand up against the saboteur. Once the behavior has been verified, the saboteur should be calmly confronted (one-on-one) to make sure he understands the facts, giving him a chance to cease his activity. Sometimes, calmly alerting him that you are aware of his activity will be sufficient to stop it.

FIRO-B: A Composite View

Psychologist William Schutz, in his FIRO-B (Fundamental Interpersonal Relations Orientations-Behavior) approach, recommends analyzing interpersonal dynamics by breaking the behaviors into three basic categories—Inclusion, Control, and Affection. Further, each of these three categories can be subdivided into two other categories—wanted behavior and expressed behavior.

Inclusion refers to the need to be part of the group, to be included in group activities, and to be viewed as a member of the team. Group members who are high in wanted inclusion are those who have a high need to be part of the group, while those who are low in wanted inclusion have very little desire to be an active member or to be part of the team. Expressed inclusion is represented by actual behavior, with members who are high in expressed inclusion being those who are most involved in group activities. Trouble can develop if there is a discrepancy between wanted and expressed behavior. A member with a high desire for inclusion, but who feels they are not included in enough group activities, will end up feeling slighted by the rest of the group. Conversely, a member with a low desire for inclusion will resent efforts which require them to expand their expressed inclusion behavior.

Control is the power dimension of FIRO-B. Group members who are high on wanted control are those who want to be in positions of leadership and in positions which allows them to make decisions. Those who are low on wanted control would prefer for others to make group decisions. Again, problems can arise if there is a discrepancy between wanted and expressed control. Group members who want more power may concentrate their efforts on getting that power, with power attainment becoming a goal unto itself. The result can hurt overall group productivity. Conversely, members who are placed in leadership positions but who don't want those positions may prove to be ineffective. They will shift and delay necessary decisions, hoping somebody else will take that element away from them.

Affection is the "liking" dimension of interpersonal relationships, i.e., that area related to friendship and love. Some people have a high desire for others to like them, while others seem not to care. Such orientations can again affect group processes, particularly if there is a discrepancy between wanted and expressed behavior. Members who are high on affections needs, but low on the expression of those needs, may feel frustrated by their participation in the group based upon their perception that they are not liked or appreciated.

At first glance, High and Low behaviors (both wanted and expressed) appear to be bi-polar opposites, since they appear at two ends of a continuum. Schutz says that is merely a perception created by the continuum. Instead, he argues, there is very little difference between high and low behaviors. Both types have the same basic problem—insecurity about that particularly dimension—but they cope with it in opposite ways.

Most people fall somewhere in the middle on all three dimensions. In terms of Inclusion, for example, most people want to be included in group activities on some occasions, but want to spend time alone on others. Most people want most people to like them, but don't expect everyone to do so. And most people are willing to make some decisions for the group, but prefer not to make all of them. These mid-range needs are more conducive to balanced FIRO orientations, i.e., situations in which a person's wanted behavior corresponds to their expressed behavior, they will be satisfied with their interpersonal orientations. Such balanced situations produce the most productive group activities.

Summary

A number of interpersonal elements affect group communication and productivity. These include many perceptual and image variables as similarity, credibility, and interpersonal attraction. Each of these concepts refers to a perception that one person in the group may have of other group members. Perceived similarity evaluations can be made quickly, and these will then affect member perceptions of others credibility and interpersonal attraction. Interpersonal attraction, particularly in terms of task attraction, is an important component in making the group experience a positive one.

Sometimes overlooked, however, is the extent to which personality variables influence group behavior. Such behaviors can be disruptive to the group process, particularly when such elements as needs for inclusion, control, and affection come into play.

Perceptual and personality differences can eventually lead to group conflict. When conflict gets out of control, it becomes harder for the group to survive in a productive manner.

References

Dilenschneider, R. L. (1997). *The critical 14 years of your professional life.* New York: Birch Lane Press.

Heilbrun, C. G. (1989). *Writing a woman's life.* New York: Ballantine.

Korda, M. (1975). *Power.* New York: Ballantine.

Schutz, W. (1958). *FIRO: A three-dimensional theory of interpersonal behavior.* New York: Holt, Rinehart.

Thompson, G., & Pearce, P.F. (1992, May). The team-trust game. *Training & Development, 46,* 42-43.

Wilmot, W. W., & Hocker, J. L. (2000). *Interpersonal conflict* (6th Ed.). New York: McGraw Hill.

SOMETHING TO THINK ABOUT

1. The Non-Productive Group Member
Your group has been assigned a project, due at the end of the month. Most of your group members have done their part, but one person is always late for meetings and—if they show up—hasn't completed their assignment. Considering this situation?

    1. How would this make you feel? Why?

    2. What specific behaviors would bother you the most?

    3. How should the rest of the team address the problem?

    4. When the project is completed, the entire group will get credit (or blame) for its success (or failure). Is this fair? What can you do about it?

2. Meetingless Mondays
First there was "Casual Fridays" and now many companies are starting "Meetingless Mondays." These are days set aside for employees to reestablish personal and professional boundaries and concentrate on their own work without the interruption of meetings.

    1. Do you think this is a good idea?

    2. Are we meeting with each other too much?

    3. Do you think you could cut yourself off from meeting with your coworkers and peers for one day a week? This would include face-to-face and electronic meetings?

    4. Is the concept of personal or private business becoming obsolete?

3. Listening
One of the biggest barriers to effective listening is our tendency to engage in private planning. Private planning is when we are thinking about what we want to say, rather than listening to the other person. Given the free flowing dynamic of small group communication this is an easy listening trap to fall into.

    1. Do you find yourself private planning when you should be listening?

    2. Do you believe this happens more in groups or less in groups?

    3. Is there any way to stop private planning?

    4. What other barriers to listening are particularly relevant during meetings?

CHAPTER 4

APPROACHES TO GROUP PROBLEM SOLVING

Years ago, an advertisement in the back of cheap magazines illustrated a sure-fire bug killer. Send in $4.95, the ad claimed, and they would send you a sure-fire bug killer, one that worked first time and every time. When the package arrived, the naive buyer opened the box and found two blocks of wood and a simple sheet of instructions. "Place bug on Block A. Hit Block A with Block B"—a sure-fire method that always worked. The problem, of course, was getting the bug to stay on Block A long enough to hit it.

Proponents of group problem solving methods have a similar problem. Several different techniques for solving problems have been suggested. Most follow logical and progressive techniques that sound as if they should work. When placed into a real-world environment, though, group participants often find they have trouble staying focused on the problem under consideration. Group members, most of them untrained in problem solving techniques, start arguing about tangents, prematurely jump in with proposed solutions that have not received enough thought, or shift to irrelevant topics that reflect their personal agenda instead of the problem facing the group. The result: group problem solving can become chaotic, regardless of how orderly and systematic the discussion is planned to be. This chapter will attempt to reduce the chaos of such discussions, while remembering that such elements can never be totally eliminated.

Purposeful Meetings

Meetings are scheduled for a variety of reason: *dissemination or sharing of information, delegating tasks, decision making,* or *problem-solving.* Recognizing the goal of the meeting is necessary for the group to proceed efficiently. A prepared group leader will usually inform the group members about the purpose of the meeting ahead of time, but that's not always the case. Frequently participants are not aware of the purpose or goal of the meeting until they arrive, if even then. Common complaints about meetings with unclear goals sound like this: "We go around and around and never accomplish anything," "No one seems to know what we're doing here," or "Another meeting, another waste of time."

At the beginning of every meeting, the chair should state the goal or purpose of the meeting (even if everyone has already been told) so that all group members will "be on the same page." If there is not a designated leader, then the group shares responsibility for getting started. Someone should take the initiative and ask the group about the perceived goal of the meeting. Then a discussion can follow with all members arriving at a defined goal together.

Information Sharing

Meetings that have a goal of information sharing leaves the individual member with the task of deciding whether he or she is the recipient or the supplier of the desired information, or possibly both. If a supervisor simply has information to share with a specific group, a memo would be more appropriate than a meeting. In that case, calling a meeting could invite trouble. If a meeting is scheduled, discussion is expected, and some participants may attack the information. If discussion on the information is needed, each member should be forewarned so that they may be prepared to contribute pertinent data. When that information is exchanged among the members, the goal is reached and the meeting should be adjourned. Thus, the meeting time should be directly related to the amount of information that should be disseminated. By focusing on the goal of the meeting, the members can help keep the length of the meeting to a minimum.

Delegation of Tasks

Meetings that have a purpose of delegating tasks are usually called to make sure that all jobs that produce the organization's specific product will get done by someone. With a task, there is no doubt about what is to be done or how to go about doing it. It's just a matter of who is going to do it. If a boss wants certain individuals to do certain tasks, a meeting is not justified. Such assignments can be made without necessitating a group discussion. But scheduling a meeting to solicit volunteers for specific tasks is common. A listing of the tasks followed by individuals volunteering to do the tasks accomplishes the purpose of the meeting, and it can then be adjourned.

Decision Making

If a supervisor needs help in deciding who should be assigned to different tasks, she may then call a meeting of fellow supervisors to discuss recommendations. The purpose of the meeting has shifted, though; it is not longer a task delegation meeting, but one with a goal of making a decision. Decision making can be defined as a process of making reasoned choices from several alternatives. If the choices are clear, the discussion results in a decision, or series of decisions, fairly quickly. The meeting has served its purpose and can be adjourned.

Problem-Solving

Unfortunately, decisional choices are not always easy. Sometimes, none of the alternatives seem acceptable. When that occurs, the group has a blocked goal, or problem. A goal is a human desire toward which one is willing to work. A small group goal is a human desire toward which all group members are willing to work. Problems arise when there is indecision on how to proceed to overcome barriers that prevent attainment of an agreed-upon goal. A problem is a question of what should be done, and how (Smith, 1965). Thinking about a problem is difficult for individuals, but the complexity is multiplied for groups. Unless the group agrees upon (1) the nature of the problem and (2) some order for discussing the problem, arriving at a solution will be both time consuming and often unproductive. The remainder of this chapter will offer some suggestions for seeking consensus on these two elements—types of discussion questions and problem-solving agendas.

Types of Discussion Groups

One reason the problem-solving bug keeps jumping off the block is that different group members will approach the same issue from different perspectives. Different types of questions are discussed in different ways; if group members differ in their perception of the nature of a problem, their discussions will also diverge and scatter along several directions. The first step in stopping that type of chaos is to recognize the type of question being faced by the group. At the problem-solving level, groups can face three different types of questions—questions of fact, value, or policy.

Questions of Fact

Questions of fact deal with whether something is or is not the case. Typically, questions of fact can be answered much like a student would responds to a "true-false" or "yes-no" test in that there is usually a right answer that can eventually be identified. For example, "Who was the first American to step on the Moon?" can be answered accurately—"Neil Armstrong." Questions of this nature often require only that the group conduct research and gather relevant information before attempting to reach a final conclusion. The answers to many questions of fact are already known to someone else; the group's task in these situations may essentially become one of finding a credible source for the information.

But not all questions of fact are easily answered. "Does God exist?" is a question of fact, but not necessarily one that's easily answered. Theologians have toiled for centuries to come up with definitive arguments for both sides of that debate. Conversely, "Who was the 16th president of the United States?" is a relatively easy question of fact. Even for those who might not know the answer (Abraham Lincoln) off the top of their head, all that is required to find the answer is a little research. Group problem solving is relatively useless in this type of question, since resolution is more of a task than a problem. That is, almost any one member can discover the answer without group deliberation.

Questions of Value

Questions of value are often more complex. They require the group to assess the relative worth of some idea or object. Such evaluations can occur along a number of dimensions—good or bad, right or wrong, pretty or ugly. Regardless of the dimension measured, though, the ultimate goal of the group is to make a decision on the relative merit of the questions. The complexity of questions of value can vary tremendously. At one basic level, questions of value are the essential questions faced by committees that must decide which particular actor is worthy of an Emmy or Oscar nomination or which baseball player is worthy of the annual Most Valuable Player Award. But philosophers also debate questions of value ("Is God just?), and some of these questions continue to elude definitive answers.

Resolving questions of value typically depends upon success at two discussion elements: (1) agreeing on the questions of facts which are the foundation of the value, and (2) establishing some criteria for evaluating the value. Both elements can sometimes be difficult to do. Group members may assume that everyone shares their understanding of the facts; if so, they might be reluctant to spend the necessary time to go over those items. Similarly, group members may also be reluctant to establish value-laden criteria, since such discussions might call into question the criteria behind their own value system. Either way, questions of value can be difficult issues for groups to face.

Questions of Policy

Questions of policy focus on decisions regarding what should or should not be done. Policy questions require decisions about possible actions—"Should more money be spent on education?" "What should be done about reducing the cost of medical care in the United States?" Questions of policy are those which are most frequently addressed by group problem-solving discussions. They are frequently complicated in nature, with the discussion having to operate at multiple levels of analysis. Often both questions of facts and questions of value must be resolved before an answer can be reached on a question of policy. Sometimes, though, group members have trouble distinguishing a question of policy from the relevant value questions related to it. The above question about education, for example, assumes that there are positive values associated with "education" as a concept. If some group members don't share that value, then the discussion may progress in an unproductive manner.

Problem-Solving Agendas

To provide more guidance for group discussions—regardless of which type of question might arise—several scholars have attempted to provide an agenda or checklist to help guide such discussions. A number of different ideas have been suggested for following a logical and orderly discussion of group problems. We will examine (1) the Classic Reflective Thinking Model, (2) some modern variations of that approach, and (3) some other approaches that view group problems from a different perspective.

The Classic Reflective Thinking Model

William Smith's (1965) original classic work on group problem solving was based almost entirely on the classic Reflective Thinking Model.

This approach to group discussion took the reflective thinking process described by John Dewey (1933) and applied it to the group environment. Depending upon which version is used, this approach breaks the discussion process into a series of six or seven steps. The process is effective when the leader and group members have some training in the method and are willing to work toward a common goal. It works best in a group of three-to-eight people but can be rather time consuming, committing the group to a series of meetings.

The advantage of this approach is that it can build consensus by involving all group members in the decision. As the group discusses the problem in each step of the process, it is working toward a solution that takes into account different perceptions and different areas of expertise among the group members. A series of decisions will be made together. The initial steps allow the group to decide if the problem warrants further discussion. Each step paves the way for agreement on the solution. If the group reaches a final decision by consensus, the solution will be supported long after the discussion is over, and thus have a better chance of being implemented (Hickson & Stacks, 1998).

Groups who use this approach should think of problem solving as an open-ended inquiry. This dictates that the group members adopt an investigative posture, a mind set of openness, and a willingness to look at all possibilities. The group spends much of their time posing questions to each other and providing answers. Personal agendas and preconceived ideas of the solution are minimized. The group goal becomes preeminent.

How is this achieved? Communication experts differ in their adaptations of Dewey's approach, but this six-step process is a common version.

1. *Define the problem.* The Reflective Thinking Model requires the group to define the nature of the problem at the outset of the discussion. Preferably, the question should be defined as an open-ended, unbiased policy question. An open-ended question ("What should be the government's policy on providing health care for the elderly?") allows for discussion of more options that does a closed-ended question ("Is the approach of the Democrats or the Republicans the more effective way to address health care issues?"). The latter limits the discussion to only two alternatives, while the first allows for the inclusion of multiple options.

A key element of defining the problem is the definition of key terms. For the group to be successful, all group members must share a common understanding of the topic. In the above question, for example, definition of "elderly" would be important. What age group constitutes "elderly"? Does it refer to those over age 60, 65, or 72? If agreement on that definition is not reached initially, it will create problems later in the discussion.

Definition of the problem also involves defining the scope of the problem. The scope must be narrowed to a manageable level. The authors have seen too many group projects, done as class assignments, unravel because the group took on more than it could handle within one semester. At the same time, a problem that is defined too narrowly becomes worthless. Something that is too easy to solve or too easy to accomplish may not be worth a group effort.

2. *Analyze the problem.* In the second step, the group looks at the scope of the problem and its importance. However, such analysis requires information. Before a group can effectively discuss the issues relevant to any specific problem, the members must have accurate and reliable information. Before proceeding with any discussion of possible solutions, Smith recommended that the group interrupt the discussion process until enough information could be obtained so that the members could fully understand the causes and effects (symptoms) of the problem. Who is affected besides the group? Will the situation improve itself or become worse if nothing is done?

Group members should examine the history of the problem to better understand how it has developed in the present. What has been done previously, if anything, to solve the problem? Was it effective? What barriers hindered previous efforts at solving the problem? An understanding of how a problem has developed and how it has been addressed in the past can provide cues for limiting its expansion in the future.

The analysis stage of group discussion is essentially a research stage. At the corporate level, some companies hire research specialists to gather this information for them. In smaller companies or organizations, though, this function is often part of the group role. In those instances, care must be taken to assure the accuracy of the information. As one consultant told the authors, "If the research is good, your job is easy. But bad information makes everything worse. I'd rather have no information than bad information. Bad information almost always guarantees a bad decision."

Volkema and Gorman (1998) describe the first two steps as the *formulation of the problem.* Gathering information to define or describe the perceived problem is essential in preventing a group from committing an "error of the third kind," i.e., solving the wrong problem (Yadav, 1985). Groups that exhibit substantial formulation activity have more efficient problem-solving experiences and make better decisions. Groups have a tendency to rush through these phases because they erroneously assume that everyone already understands the problem; such groups narrow the scope of the problem and focus on solutions prematurely (Volkema, 1995). It is tempting to jump to a discussion of solutions because the cause-and-effect relationship between the goal and the barriers often reveals what should be done. For the reflective thinking model to work, though, the group must be willing to invest the time and self-discipline to effectively and thoroughly utilize these first two steps. A group will be more likely to agree on a solution for a problem if it first understands the problem.

3. *Establish criteria for solutions.* Most aspects of Dewey's Reflective Thinking Model simply represent an organization of thought processes that most qualified group members would use anyway—whether they were trained in problem solving or not. The concepts of defining and analyzing the problem are hardly new and understanding them will add little to the problem solving skills of those who are already effective. But the third stage—criteria development—represents an area that many novice group members will overlook in their standard attempts at group problem solving. *Criteria are guidelines, boundaries, standards or rules that a group agrees to follow in reaching a solution to their problem.* Establishing criteria is a crucial stage, and one that often makes the difference between a good or a bad decision. The criteria stage is the point at which the group members develop the standards for evaluating possible solutions. If done properly, the effective use of discussion during this stage makes the rest of the discussion relatively easy and free of negative conflict. Setting criteria helps the group to be unbiased and objective about proposed solutions (Hamilton, 1997). Groups that have a clear standard for their decisions have a chance for a more effective process and a superior solution (Graham, Papa & McPherson, 1997).

The main task here is relatively simple—identifying and prioritizing those factors that must be considered before making a final decision. This might include costs, time, resources, personal consideration, ethical considerations, and legal considerations. If such elements are discussed in advance, many potentially ineffective or unacceptable solutions can be dismissed quickly from later discussion.

If these factors are omitted, however, every group member will tend to respond to any suggested solution in terms of their own, unarticulated value system. Consider, for example, a local club that wants to implement a new fund-raising drive for charity. A suggestion that the club sell raffle tickets might be acceptable to most group members, but one member may seem to stubbornly hold out against it. One possibility: the "holdout" may object to raffles on moral grounds, believing they are to similar to legalized gambling, but feel reluctant to express such mild moral opinions in front of a group that otherwise seems to like the idea. Or, even worse, the member may reluctantly accept the idea while never voicing their concerns; the raffle decision will be affirmed, but that member may never actively participate in ensuring that it becomes successful.

4. *Propose solutions.* Finally, the group gets to talk about proposed solutions—something they've wanted to do from the beginning of the discussion. The goal of this stage is to identify as many alternatives as possible. As each proposal is made, it is evaluated in terms of the criteria developed in stage three. Will the proposal raise the amount of money that was the goal of the campaign? Can it do this within a reasonable time? Is the work load required within the capability of the group members?

The goal at this point is a long list of possibilities, not a list of high quality solutions (Smith, 1965). One way to achieve this is through a process known as **brainstorming**, a technique that encourages all members to think freely and contribute a range of options. Brainstorming is a method of suggesting ideas quickly and spontaneously in random order until ideas are exhausted. Members of the group stimulate each other's imaginations and build on each other's ideas. All members should participate, with someone compiling a list of all suggestions. Later, the list can be reviewed and categorized for further discussion. For effective brainstorming, the group refrains from judging each solution as it is made; members are more likely to contribute if they know their ideas won't be shot down immediately. Research has shown that the quality of both individual and group decisions are improved when open exchanges are allowed (Burleson, Levine & Samter, 1984).

Another approach for generating proposed solutions is the **Nominal Group Technique**, or NGT (Delbecq, 1986). In this approach, solutions are silently generated by each member and written down privately. The secretary then records one idea from each member until all ideas are one the board, including ones thought of while others were talking. Each member then privately selects the top five or six ideas and ranks them according to preference. Votes are recorded and the group selects the top ideas.

5. Analyze solutions and select the best. The group may find that as they evaluate each proposed solution that this step of the process is easier than expected. They already have a clear understanding of the causes of the problem, barriers to the goal, a wide range of options, and a criteria for the solutions. The ground work has been laid.

The list of possible solutions is discussed in terms of the strengths and weaknesses of each. As each proposal is evaluated, it is either discarded or retained for future consideration—based on the extent to which it meets the established criteria. Further, all possible alternatives must be evaluated. A potential problem here is that once a solution is found that meets the criteria, the group may feel satisfied and think their job is done. It's not. They need to continue discussing other possibilities. Even though one solution is found that meets the minimum criteria for the group, another may be waiting in the wings which is even more effective. Unless the discussion continues, it will not be found.

Because problems are complicated, solutions may range from outright removal of a barrier to the solution, or cause of the problem, or to the revision of the goal in light of an immovable barrier. During this process, a positive mentality should be maintained. Researchers have found it important to positively evaluate decision alternatives instead of quickly eliminating them off the list. When group members focus on the positive characteristics of decision alternatives, a more constructive climate for interaction occurs. Unfortunately, groups often go immediately to a "process of elimination" and often overlook the potential of some solutions (Graham, Papa, & McPherson, 1997).

If the discussion has been effective, when the discussion reaches this state, many group members have already figured out what the best solution will be. All that remains is for the group as a whole to affirm that decision. Again, a mistake can occur here if the discussion is stopped too soon. A full discussion of the chosen solution, at this point in the process, allows all group members to become participants in the final decision. If you stop talking too soon, that won't happen. During the earlier discussion stage, some members would have been advocates of other ideas—ideas that were eventually discarded by the group. To implement the solution (the next stage), the group is going to need the involvement and commitment of all group members. A thorough discussion of the selected solution allows the group to re-unite for that purpose.

6. *Develop a plan to implement the solution.* For some problems, the implementation procedure is clear because it is implied in the solution chosen. For others, implementation is really an organizational problem—not something directly associated with group decision making. In those cases, implementing the solution may become the biggest difficulty. A satisfied group may take their decision to upper management and be met with a "who's going to pay for it" response. Still, the group can increase the chances of its solution working by taking an active role in the implementation process. Thus, before adjourning, the group should (1) identify the resources needed for the project, (2) assign individuals to take responsibility for implementing the various components of the plan, (3) establish deadlines for completion of the initial tasks, and (4) articulate a feedback and evaluation process that ensures the project is proceeding on schedule. Those four key elements—*resources, responsibilities, deadlines,* and *evaluations*—will be crucial to the success of the project.

Modern Variations
The Reflective Thinking model has a number of strengths. Among the most obvious are (1) it prescribes and organized approach to a problem, (2) makes group members more conscious of the group process, and (3) can save time (Jensen, 1991, p. 30). However, there are also a number of problems associated with the technique.

One is that the approach works effectively only if every group member is trained in the process. The time-saving advantage of the agenda, for example, is dependent upon all participants adhering to the agenda set down by the model. Untrained members are frequently unwilling to do so.

Second, although the model takes a highly logical approach to problem solving (and that is an asset), it essentially ignores the interpersonal elements associated with social interactions. The individual feelings, attitudes, and egos of the participants are not considered.

A third problem with the Reflective Thinking Model is that it encourages participants to delay their thinking about proposed solutions. While that increases the effectiveness of the process, it goes against natural conversational tendencies of many group members. Many group members are eager to voice their suggestions, and they want to do so early in the process. The Reflective Thinking Model somewhat stifles this trend by imposing structure on group discussions. Many group members, though, will find this structure to be an artificial one, and some groups will resist using it. Research has shown that groups involved in problem-solving discussions typically go through three distinct phases which roughly correspond to the seven steps of the Reflective Thinking Model, but they do not necessarily follow the model in exact sequential order (Bales & Strodtbeck, 1951).

Instead, discussions typically open with an *orientation* stage in which members ask for and exchange information; this information is then classified, confirmed, and repeated by the members until they move into the second stage. In the second stage—*evaluation*—the group discusses members' opinions and express their personal feelings about the problem. In the third stage, *control,* the group members ask for and exchange suggestions and discuss possible solutions before making a decision. While these three stages cover most of the same areas as that of the Reflective Thinking Model, they might not get covered in quite as orderly a manner as proponents of the method might prefer.

In addition, unless each of the discussion participants has been well trained in the process, some group members are likely to diverge from the discussion agenda. And finally, the entire process may be overly structured anyway. Dewey's original discussion of the reflective thinking process noted that all of the steps needed to be completed to be successful; however, he did not specify that each step had to be completed in any specific order. As long as all steps in the process are covered—regardless of the order in which they are covered—the group should come up with a workable solution. Other problem solving agendas have been offered which take advantage of this factor. These two approaches are the *Ideal Solution Form* and the *Single Question Form.*

Both the Ideal Solution Form and the Single Question Form have the advantage of letting group members talk about solutions early—something they naturally move toward anyway. Both approaches offer a more natural progression of group discussion than is found in the Reflective Thinking Model. Eventually, too, both forms meet the primary requirements that are established in the Reflective Thinking model, albeit in a different chronological sequence. Further, both approaches have the advantage of being workable with relatively little training on the part of the group members. All that is required for them to be effective is the presence of one trained person with leadership skills who will ask the right questions at the right time.

The Ideal Solution Form. The Ideal Solution format (Larson, 1969, p. 453) is a simple process which allows groups to talk about solutions early in the process. The key question in the format is the second one: "What is the Ideal Solution for all parties involved?" Although phrased as a "solution," the question really generates a set of criteria that serves to evaluate all subsequent proposals.

A list of proposals is generated by the third question in the process: "What are the options available to us?" As each proposal is offered, the group can evaluate it in terms of the criteria generated by the ideal solution. That leads to the decisional stage: "Of the solutions available, which one comes closest to the ideal solution?"

The Ideal Solution Form can be particularly useful on questions of policy or questions of value. Identification of the ideal solution establishes the standards that policy decisions must meet and allows group members to articulate their personal values in terms of the topic at hand. Further, it is relatively easy to use. Only one person in the group has to be familiar with the approach. By asking the initial "Ideal Solution" question, that person can often direct the flow of the conversation—even if they are not the formal leader of the group. All that is required is the introduction of the questions as suggestions for the group. In effect, the Ideal Solution Form is an effective and non-intrusive way for members to increase group productivity.

Its weakness is that group members are not compelled to use it. Further, since—by its nature—the approach is non-intrusive, other group members may over-ride attempts to use it by continuing to articulate their own personal agenda. Such dominance by other group members do not eliminate the potential for it to be effective, but it can be a definite barrier.

The Single Question Form. Johnny drives from Birmingham to Montgomery at the rate of 70 miles per hour. He then drives from Montgomery to Mobile at the rate of 80 miles per hour. The distance from Montgomery to Birmingham is 135 miles. The distance from Mobile to Montgomery is 160 miles. Question: How long does it take Johnny to drive from Birmingham to Mobile?

The Single Question Form (Larson, 1969, p. 453) is particularly effective at solving such questions of facts. The Single Question Form uses the single-question format to define the problem. Identification of the sub-questions is a means of analyzing the problem. Identifying the sub-questions provides a means of breaking the problem into smaller tasks, some of which can be handled by individual members.

In the above example, the single question that must be answered in the amount of time that it takes Johnny to drive from Birmingham to Mobile. That question, in turn, can be broken down into two sub-questions—Johnny's driving time from (1)Birmingham to Montgomery and (2) from Montgomery to Mobile. Gathering the information on each sub-question reveals that it took Johnny 1.5 hours for the first segment (135 miles/70 mph) and 2 hours for the second segment (160/80). The final answer: Johnny made the trip in three-and-a-half hours. The Single Question Form places an emphasis on analysis of data by breaking the project down into discreet elements. A large problem that seems insurmountable often becomes more workable when divided into a series of small questions.

Special Cases

Force Field Analysis. Force Field Analysis views a problem by analyzing it within its context. There is no pre-set agenda for group members to follow, but there is a suggested orderly process that must be completed. It is relatively simple and flexible, however, allowing group members to jump from one part of the discussion to another as they happen to think of ideas. The basic approach is to compile two lists (see Figure 4.1) a list of *helping forces* and (2) *holding forces*. Helping forces are those factors which exist within the environment which are either already contributing or could contribute to have a positive impact on the problem. Holding forces are those factors which exist within the environment which contribute to the problem, or have the potential to make it worse.

Helping Forces	Holding Forces
1.	1.
2.	2.
3.	3.
4.	4.
5.	5.

Figure 4.1 Force Field Analysis Form

After a list has been compiled, the group examines each item with a dual screening process. The first step is to distinguish between those factors which can be influenced by the group and those which are beyond their control. Those beyond the control of the group are eliminated, and the discussion focuses on those factors that they could potentially influence.

Each relevant factor is then examined individually, with group members looking for ways to increase the positive impact of the helping forces while limiting or eliminating the negative impact of the holding forces. For example, suppose that a committee was asked to make suggestions for increasing attendance at the annual performance by a local symphony. One of the possible "holding forces" for such attendance might be scheduling conflicts with other entertainment venues. If so, the impact of that holding force could be reduced by re-scheduling the annual performance.

Buzz Sessions. A buzz session is a small group drawn from a larger audience that discusses a specific element of a larger discussion topic (Phillips, 1948). Suppose that a group of 50 salesmen had gathered at a convention to discuss a recent downturn in sales. Rather than having the entire group discuss the entire problem at once—a situation that could quickly get out of control—the chairman of the meeting could divide the group into several smaller groups to discuss specific aspects of the problem. One group might focus on stock market trends that were affecting sales. Another might look at the impact of foreign competition. A third may discuss the potential for on-line competition. The list could be continued based upon the nature of the problem under discussion.

Buzz groups are effective at encouraging member participation, and they are particularly effective at drawing out participation from members who might be intimidated by large crowds. To be effective, however, the leader should have a list of potential discussion topics prepared in advance. Trying to develop such topics "off the cuff" typically results in an uneven distribution of discussion sub-topics. Some end up being created just to give the members something to do while contributing little to the topic itself. That can be avoided if the sub-divisions are created in advance.

Phillips 66 is a variation of a buzz session that focuses on questions. The term refers to a small group whose function is to develop questions about an area of a problem. The name comes from dividing a large group into smaller, six-member groups who discuss an issue for six minutes. It is most useful in those situations in which the primary discussion group involves a large number of members. The procedure is simple. First, the audience is divided into smaller groups of three-to-eight members (ideal size, six). Second, a chairman is appointed for each group, and a time limit (usually 6-10 minutes) is established for the discussion period. Third, the group uses that time to develop questions dealing with the discussion topic. At the end of the time period, the chairman presents the group's questions to the primary discussion group.

Phillips 66 is particularly useful for encouraging member participation in a large group. Since it focuses on questions, not answers, it delves into areas in which each member can participate. And, it allows the raising of questions that concern group members—questions that might be suppressed in the larger group setting.

Quality Circles. Quality circles developed as a workplace technique in Japan that encouraged workers to make suggestions for improving the quality of their product or service. Juran (1976, p. 15) defined a quality circle as "a small group of departmental work leaders and line operators who have volunteered to spend time outside of their regular hours to help solve departmental quality problems." The process generally works best when the participants are skilled workers who understand the product and the process and may range in size from three to fifteen members. Quality Circles have the potential to make two distinct contributions to the quality of the work product. First, by constantly evaluating and look for ways to improve quality, the group can make specific and effective suggestions to the production process. Second, the very existence of the group, along with its constant presence in the workplace, serves to elevate awareness of quality as a goal for the group.

Delphi Technique. The Delphi Technique is a procedural approach to problem solving that is designed for the introduction of a wide variety of ideas and evaluating the merits of each. It also has the advantage of being a workable process even when participants are not physically in the same place—it can all be accomplished with the exchange of data by mail or by e-mail. The process begins with each member collecting and submitting ideas. A central organizer (a leader of a secretary) compiles the lists, synthesizes similar ideas, and develops an integrated list of all the suggested options. This list is then returned to the participants who then rank or rate each suggestion. This process can be repeated a number of times, with untenable ideas eliminated and strong ones put up for further evaluation.

Choosing Solutions

Consensus. Regardless of which problem solving approach is used, the ultimate goal of a problem solving group is to develop a solution for the problem. Typically what happens is that a number of alternative solutions are proposed. Ideally, when that occurs, the final solution is based on some comparison between the attributes of each proposal as compared to the criteria developed by the group. As the issue is discussed, each group member starts to realize that one particular solution is superior to the others. By the end of the discussion, all group members are in agreement is to what the solution should be.

Realistically, though, that doesn't always happen. Almost invariably, some group members will make a different assessment regarding the alternative proposals, with each believing that their proposal offers the best chance of a positive solution. When those types of stalemates develop, reaching consensus on a solution may be difficult. If so, alternative ways of choosing the solution have to be considered. These include (1) voting, (2) ranking, (3) weighting, (4) and the nominal group technique.

Voting. The group may simply choose the solution that is favored by most of the group's members. This element of majority rule has the advantage of choosing the most popular option while simultaneously demonstrating to the minority that they are a minority. The vote allows them to express their opinion (even if it is a losing one), and their willingness to go along with the vote ensures that they have participated in the process. Still, voting does not ensure that the best option will be selected—only that the most popular one will. When groups make decisions on the basis of popular vote, they often have to be prepared to shift options later on if the solution should prove untenable.

Ranking. Ranking is a process of multiple voting. Instead of voting on their top solution, the members are asked to rank each option beginning with "1" (the best) down to ever how many options are under consideration. Someone then tallies the scores, with those options receiving the lowest scores (i.e., high ranks) being retained for further consideration.

Weighting. Weighting, much like ranking, involves the assignment of some mathematical principle to the various options. Unlike ranking, though, individuals are not required to discriminate between each option. Someone who found two options highly acceptable, for example, could give equally high ratings to each one. Again, the final tallies decide which options will be retained for further consideration.

Nominal Group Technique. The nominal group technique (Delbecq, Van de Ven, & Gustafson, 1975; Huseman, 1977) is a four-step process which can be used when groups become stalemated over a number of possible options. It combines aspects of written suggestions, verbal interactions, and numerical voting procedures. Each member is asked to silently generate ideas (usually in written form). These ideas are then recorded in a round-robin fashion, ensuring that everyone's ideas have been presented. These ideas are then discussed in a open forum, which is then followed by a preliminary vote. If necessary, the top suggestions can be the focus of further discussion, followed by another vote.

Summary

The study of group problem solving can become somewhat confusing. Students must learn to distinguish between questions of fact, value and policy. They must become acquainted with a number of different problem-solving techniques—many of which take opposing views as to what constitutes effective problem solving. Despite these factors, though, a number of common elements have emerged from the differing points of view. These common elements can be considered the "secrets" of successful group projects. Do these things, and your chances of success will increase dramatically.

1. *Make sure all or most of the group members support the project.* Group work can be tiring and frustrating under the best of conditions. Frustration can be reduced if the group, as a whole, is supportive of the group goals. But if someone within the group opposes the project, its chances of success are limited.

2. *Identify the resources needed for the group and how those resources will be obtained.* Groups can't work with 'nothin'. They will need money, information, equipment, and skills to accomplish their goal. If those resources cannot be obtained, the goal needs to be re-evaluated.

3. *Give individual members individual responsibilities.* Know who will be responsible for what. Even more important, be sure each person knows what their responsibility is.

4. *Set deadlines.* The human species is remarkably adept at procrastination. In the absence of deadlines, many members will simply

not get around to focusing on their individual responsibilities. Set deadlines, and work within those deadlines whenever possible.

5. *Verify progress.* The group leader must have a feedback and evaluation system in place that allows for monitoring the group's progress toward its goal.

6. *Have a fallback plan.* Problems will always develop. Some group members will not meet deadlines, either due to their own procrastination or due to unexpected emergencies. Either way, the group's work still has to be done. When the person who was providing the research information on the first element leaves town due to an illness in the family, somebody has to step in and fulfill their role. Remember, the goal is the successful completion of the project—not finger-pointing at those members who don't meet group expectations.

Learn these six elements and—regardless of which problem solving technique you prefer—your group is likely to be successful.

References

Bales, R.F., & Strodtbeack, F. L. (1951). Phases in group problem solving. *Journal of Abnormal and Social Psychology, 46,* 485-495.

Burleson, B. R., Levine, B. J., & Samter, W. (1984). Decision-making procedure and decision quality. *Human Communication Research, 10,* 557-574.

Delbecq, A. L., Van de Ven, A.H., & Gustafson, D. H. (1975). *Group techniques for program planning: A guide to nominal group and Delphi processes.* Glenview, IL: Scott, Foresman.

Dewey, J. (1933). *How we think: A restatement of the relation of reflective thinking to the educative process.* Boston: Heath.

Graham, E. E., Papa, M. J., & McPherson, M. B. (1997). An applied test of the functional communication perspective of small group decision-making. *Southern Communication Journal, 62,* 269-279.

Hamilton, C. (1997).*Communicating for results: A guide for business & the professions* (5th ed.). Belmont, CA: Wadsworth.

Hickson, M., III, & Stacks, D. W. (1998). *Organizational communication In the personal context: From interview to retirement.* Boston: Allyn & Bacon.

Huseman, R.C. (1977). The role of the nominal group in small group communication. In R. C. Huseman, C.M. Logue, and D.L. Freshley (Eds.), *Readings in interpersonal and organizational com-munication* (pp. 493-507), 3rd Ed. Boston: Holbrook Press.

Jensen, A. D. (1991). *Small group communication.* Belmont, CA: Wadsworth.

Juran, J. M. (1976). The QC Circle phenomenon. In D.M. Amsden & R.T. Amsden (Ed.), *QC Circles: Applications, tools, and theory.* Milwaukee: ASQC.

Larson, C. E. (1969). Forms of analysis and small group problem-solving. *Speech Monographs, 36,* 452-455.

Smith, W. S. (1965). *Group problem-solving through discussion: A process essential to democracy.* Indianapolis: Bobbs-Merrill.

Stacks, D. W., & Hocking, J. E. (1999). *Communication research* (2d ed). New York: Longman.

Volkema, R. J. (1995).Creativity in MS/OR:Managing the process of formulating the problem. *Interfaces, 25(3),* 81-87.

Volkema, R. J., & Gorman, R. H. (1998). The influence of cognitive-based group composition on decision-making process and outcome. *Journal of Management Studies, 35,* 105-117.

Yadav, S. B., & Korukonda, A. (1985). Management of type III error in problem identification. *Interfaces, 15(4),* 55-61.

CHAPTER 5

NEGOTIATION

Representatives of a labor union meet with management to discuss a change in the workers' health benefits. A young couple visits an automobile dealer, looking to purchase a new car for a growing family. An administrator summons a ten-year employee to his office to discuss a change in job assignments. Each of these situations is a prelude to a negotiation session. As Acuff (1997) noted, "We pretty much negotiate all day every day. It's asking the boss for a raise, getting six people to help us on this project from the information systems group." With increasing emphasis on teams and group work, the importance of negotiation skills has become even more critical.

Negotiation is the use of communication tactics to reach a settlement with another. Cohen (1980) defined it as "the use of information and power to affect behavior within a 'web of tension'" (p. 16). By either definition, negotiation is a rampart part of modern society, but one that is often overlooked or ignored. The latter seems to be the more common choice, because many people simply don't like the concept of negotiation. "Haggling," as some people call it, has a negative connotation to many people—to so many, in fact, that many retail businesses now advertise "No haggle" prices.

Why the negative outlook on such an important communication process? One reason is that negotiation is often presented from a win-lose perspective that is full of hidden traps for the unwary (Fuller, 1991). To engage in negotiation is to attempt to get the better of another person. Even if the negotiator is successful, their gain has come at the expense of somebody else. As a result, winning a negotiation session can be as painful for the winner as for the loser, inducing guilt that they would rather not experience. Others view negotiation as a series of compromises in which nobody wins. Person A makes an offer, B counteroffers. This process is repeated until some mid-level figure or compromise is reached, one that is at least acceptable to both but the ideal of neither. Everybody loses a little.

But, not everyone has a negative opinion of negotiation. Some thrive on it, motivated by its competitive nature. Such people are valuable assets to most organizations; they can negotiate bargains and deals which are beneficial to both themselves and their company. No wonder, then, that companies and corporations often hunt for people who are "natural" negotiators.

They never find them. Negotiation is not a "natural" skill, at all, but one that is learned through a developmental process. During childhood, everyone's negotiation skills are limited. As each person matures, however, some people develop negotiation skills while others seem to shun them.

Gender seems to be one of those developmental factors that influences attitudes toward negotiation. Males, who are generally more competitive than women, are more likely to approach negotiation as a competition. But, both males and females are likely to be more accommodating in negotiations if the other person is a female.

One common myth about negotiation is that it is a talent possessed by some but not by others. Actually, negotiation is a skill, not a talent. Further, success in negotiation is more often a by-product of preparation than of verbal jousting ability. In other words, anyone who will work at negotiation can be successful at it.

Planning for Negotiation

Some athletic coaches have an adage to emphasize the value of practice: "Failing to prepare is preparing for failure." The same axiom applies to negotiation. Successful negotiators don't wait for the face-to-face encounter to begin working. More often than not, success can be linked to the advanced preparation of the participants. Those who are better prepared have the edge.

Researching the Issue

Cohen (1980, p. 18) identified three crucial variables to negotiation: information, time, and power. A participant is at a disadvantage if the other person knows more about the participants and the issue (information), if the other side isn't under the same deadline (time), and if the other side has more authority (power). All three of these factors can be analyzed in advance of the negotiation, but the starting point is *information.* Negotiation skills are based on meticulous preparation of information related to the issue. When purchasing a car, for example, the salespeople have an edge in information. They are more likely to know the wholesale price of the car, the finance options available, and the lowest price at which the dealer can make a reasonable profit. The potential buyer who arms themselves with similar information in advance, through pre-negotiation research, is in a better position to negotiate for a bargain. In other words, successful negotiation requires that you do your homework. In a financial transaction, this means knowing an item's fair market value and how much bargaining room the other person has. In other forms of negotiation, the same rule applies—learn as much as you can about the issue and the other party's position on it.

Analyzing the Situation

Three attributes—power, time, and precedents—are parts of the situational components of negotiation. An understanding of those factors provides you with an understanding of the advantages and disadvantages that you face. Sometimes, realization of a weakness provides a cue for overcoming it.

Power discrepancies are critical. The person with the most power has an edge in any negotiation. Within an organization, the most common source of power is legitimate power, i.e.g, perceived authority that is not questioned. That places any lower level or mid-level employee at a disadvantage when dealing with a supervisor. The high-power person is in a position to block negotiation efforts, sometimes with little justification. There is little that the low-power person can do to alter that outcome, once a decision is made. But power discrepancies can be dealt with by lining up allies in advance of the meeting. Numerical support can compensate for differences in power, particularly if one of the allies is of equal or higher rank than the other party. Power even comes into play in consumer negotiations; one of the easiest ways to get a discount, for example, is to use your "clout" if you know someone who works at the retail establishment.

Time constraints can also affect negotiation. The party under the shortest deadline is at a disadvantage. The person who is under no time constraints can extend the negotiations over a longer time period, putting more pressure on the party facing a deadline to concede on some points of the issue. The time constraint is apparent even in consumer negotiations; customers often get better deals near the end of the month if a salesman is approaching a deadline short of their monthly quota. In terms of advance preparation, anything that can be done to extend your party's deadline increases your chances of a successful negotiation.

Precedents are also a factor. Within the organization, some situations typically are not open to negotiations. Others offer only limited options. Some have normative behaviors which limit the strategies that can be used. Understanding of these organizational precedents is critical, since violation of any one of them can doom the success of negotiations.

Analyzing the Opposition

"Successful negotiation lies in finding out what the other side really wants and showing them a way to get it, while you get what you want" (Cohen, p. 161). Seeking such common interests requires that part of the advance preparation should be to find out as much as possible about the other side. To be successful, you must build up rapport and trust with the other person. That requires an understanding of the other party's needs and anticipating concerns.

Typically, differences of opinions on an issue stem from one of three areas: (1) differences in information, (2) differences in experiences, or (3) differences in roles. The first component, information, can be handled with adequate research. Without adequate research, each participant will enter the negotiation with a different base of information. Advanced research can close that information gap, and having the same information that the other party has will enable you to better understand their position. Differences in experiences are harder to decipher, particularly if you do not know the other person well, but such factors can play a vital role. Experience colors a person's outlook on their position and also the other person's position, and each party sees negotiation though that biased view. Rather than seeing the issue objectively, each sees it from their own experience. A person who has had a negative experience with a previous plan is less likely to accept a similar plan again, even if it is the logical choice.

Within organizations divergent views revolve around differences in organizational roles. An administrator, whose primary role is to obtain resources for their department, is likely to always be in a constant state of negotiation with a supervisor who is concerned with controlling costs. An understanding of those role discrepancies can make the negotiations easier. One way to counter this problem is with practice sessions of role playing. Having a co-worker act out the role of the other participant can lead to an increased understanding of their position and why they hold that position. Sometimes the role playing process gets beyond the organizational role, perhaps giving cues to the experiential opposition of the other party.

The Game Plan

After completing the preparation stage, you should have enough information to develop an overall game plan for negotiation. The game plan should include (1) arguments supported by information, (2) trade-offs to be offered, and (3) trust building.

The arguments will be based on the research gathered, with some of the supporting information prepared for use in the negotiation and some withheld for strategic purposes. Arguments should be established based on the needs of the other person, rather than your own. That may sound like a simple idea, but it's rarely followed. Most novice negotiators develop their arguments from their own perspective and their own needs. It's more effective to explain why compliance on the part of the other person is a benefit to them, not to yourself. Such information is often more useful if it is in some tangible format—a chart, list, graph, etc. Other parties are more impressed by information that can be seen; further, even if the superior agrees with your negotiation requests, they may lack the power to implement the action themselves. A tangible piece of information also provides them with supporting material for passing your information and arguments up the chain of the organization.

Some information should be withheld, and topping this list would be the trade-offs you would be willing to offer the other side. Before entering the meeting, negotiation goals should be listed and divided into three areas—(1) essential, (2) desired, and (3) trade-offs. **Essential goals** are those that you feel must be obtained from the negotiation. If these are not met, the negotiation has not been useful and you have nothing to gain by reaching an agreement with the other party. Essential goals become your last line of defense, the point at which you will not retreat or concede on any other issue.

Desired goals are points that have a high priority but are not essential; having them would benefit you and/or your group. Still, you've done without these factors in the past, and—if necessary—you could do so in the future. Desired goals become your second wall of defense; you hold on to these as long as possible, sacrificing them only if they can contribute to the attainment of all essential goals. **Trade-offs** are items that would be nice to win but which hold a low priority. These become your first wall of defense, the first things you feel you can give up and which are offered to the other party in exchange for obtaining essential and desired items. You should plan to withhold trade-offs until you reach critical junctures in the talks; surrendering something too early makes you look like an easy target, and the other side will expect something else from you later.

Finally, before entering the talks, plan to do so with the intent of building and establishing trust with the other party. The stereotypical image of a negotiator is someone who tries to take advantage of the other party, getting as much as possible for themselves at the expense of that other person. But such results-oriented negotiation can occur only when the negotiation is a one-time event, and those are relatively rare occurrences. Most negotiations, particularly those within an organization, involve on-going relationships. Victory involves making both sides feel satisfied with the results. Aim to build trust, taking only what you need without making anybody look bad.

Cohen (1980, p. 155) calls this attitude the "lubricant demeanor," and notes that it can be engendered by trying to see the problem from the other's perspective. It also helps to trust the other person. Generally, the most trust you place in others, the more they will justify your trust. The goal is a trusting relationship in which each party has a firm belief in the honesty and reliability of the other. Trusting relationships can quickly be transformed into collaborative relationships.

The Twelve Commandments of Negotiation

Preparation of a game plan culminates in a face-to-face negotiation. Once that exchange starts, negotiation skills are largely dependent upon the individual's ability to use their prepared material, making adjustments in the presentation based on what the other person says. With this in mind, a few principles should be followed.

- *Don't get down to business immediately.* The development of the relationship is critical, so you don't immediately move into the issues at hand. Spend some time in casual talk with the other person, preferably getting them to talk about themselves. That should be relatively easy to do if the other person is someone within your organization; it takes a little more preparation for an outsider. Either way, such a casual start can provide a natural segue into a discussion of what you're trying to achieve.

- *Resist making the first offer.* Let the other person make the first move. The first offer is new information, and new information always benefits the recipient. When you counter-offer, Acuff (1997) recommends the tried-and-true method of asking for more than you want, but always keep it reasonable. Your counter-offer shapes the perception of the other side, defining the latitude of the negotiation for them. Thus that counter-offer has to be reasonable; if it doesn't make sense, negotiations will break down.

- *If money is involved, don't make opening offers in round numbers.* As McCormack (1988) noted, "Round numbers beg to be negotiated. Odd numbers sound firmer."

- *Build allies.* As Cohen (1980) noted, "No individual is an isolated entity. Everyone that you deal with is being reinforced by those around them" (p. 178). If you can gain the commitment of those around the party, that increases the incentive for them to collaborate with you.

- *Listen more than you talk.* Listening may be the toughest part of negotiation, but successful negotiation is based less on your arguments than your response to the other person's arguments. That requires careful monitoring of what they say. Encourage them to talk about their position by asking questions about their view of the issue. The more you learn about their viewpoint, the easier it will be to approach the negotiation from their perspective. That will make it easier to seek a solution which is mutually beneficial. If you understand their problem, you can craft a creative solution. At the very least, you can say, "I understand your problem. I don't know what to do, but let me think about it."

- *Don't give away unnecessary information.* A general rule here is to seek more information than you give, and that is particularly true in consumer negotiations. Still, novice negotiators often reveal more than is necessary, putting themselves at a disadvantage. Saying something positive about the product, for example, gives a salesman a slight edge in the exchange.

- *Piggyback on their ideas.* If you listen carefully, well enough to understand their position, you will find key ideas of theirs which are compatible with yours. Identify those and show how your idea can be used in conjunction with that.

- *Don't feel pressured to speak.* Silence is often interpreted as dissatisfaction with the offer. By hesitating or voicing a need to consult with others, you put more pressure on the other person to offer more. Even in consumer negotiations, silence accompanied by a small flinch can generate a better offer. Other times, merely the willingness to walk away from the negotiation is sufficient to spark another offer.

- *Be willing to take moderate risks.* Cohen (1980, p. 60) notes that "You must be willing to take risks while negotiating. If you don't take calculated chances, the other side will manipulate you." That axiom applies more to consumer negotiations than to organizational exchanges, but it still has some applicability.

- *Don't bluff.* Don't take any risks which require you to run a bluff. Professional negotiations are not poker games in which the pot goes to winner. Attempts to induce compliance by making implied threats, particularly if you have no intention of carrying out the threat, will most often fail. Before you make any threats or arguments, be sure you're willing to actually go through with them if the negotiation breaks down. If you don't, your credibility in future negotiations is ruined.

- *Don't retaliate.* At least not immediately. Fisher and Ury (1983, pp. 108-109) call this technique "negotiation jujitsu." If the other person attacks you, don't react with a counter-attack. Instead, look behind the problem to identify the reason for the attack. You can often find a need that you can satisfy, getting some concessions on your own behalf in return. The "Don't Retaliate" rule is not a hard and fast one, particularly if the other participant insists on confrontation tactics. When that occurs, a "tit-for-tat" response can be a show of strength that the other person will respect, but it must be followed by an offer that will let them return to productive negotiations while saving face.

- *Let them save face.* And that brings us to the last major point. Always let them save face. Cohen (1980, p. 193) says that

"Even when you are right, shun all opportunities to humiliate people—at least in public." A person's "face" is their public image, how they want others to see them, and any attacks on that creates problems. Included in that admonition is the advice to never ask for too much. If the disparity between the two positions is too great, offer a "bonus" item to the other person. By sweetening the deal for them, they can comply with your request without losing face. If you can do something to positive affect their public "face," that's even better. Martin Luther King, for example, used to emphasize the need to offer opponents a face-saving way to join the civil rights movement.

Negotiation Styles

Negotiation participants can approach a negotiation from two different perspectives—competition and collaboration.

Competitive Negotiation is based on a win-lose perspective. Each person negotiates on the basis of egocentric self-interest, working within a bargaining range beyond which they will not deviate. Competitive negotiations are most pronounced when there is little likelihood that the participants will have a future relationship with the other party; that's why this approach is so common in consumer negotiations, such as buying a new car. Competitive negotiations also dominate in any situation in which the negotiation is over limited resources; thus, this approach emerges during labor negotiations or in any situation in which a finite amount of money is involved. Generally, the goal for each competitive negotiator is to maximize gains within the limits of the dispute, i.e., win as much as possible during the talks, and preferably win more than the other side does.

Competitive negotiators will employ any number of communication strategies, but all are based on a common communication goal. Each negotiator tries to convince the other (1) they cannot "give" anymore, and (2) the only way to reach a settlement is for the other to give in. A number of strategies tend to emerge.

- *Each participant makes high opening demands and tries to concede slowly.* The first offers define the limits of the negotiation, establishes an estimate of the range of possibilities, and provides an indication of the other person's flexibility on the issue. In essence, this establishes the "latitude of acceptance," or at least, the "range of the negotiation."

- *When concessions are made, their value is exaggerated.* Value exaggeration occurs because it becomes an impetus for the other side to make concessions. If the value of a concession is successfully exaggerated, that puts pressure on the other side to make a concession of comparable value. Naturally, this counter concession's value is likely to be similarly exaggerated.

- *Concessions from the other side are undervalued.* Each participant tends to express dissatisfaction with what the other has offered. In consumer negotiations, a competitive buyer frequently talks about how the product doesn't meet their needs ("This isn't what I wanted") or points out blemishes ("Isn't that a scratch on the bumper"), but similar ploys are used in group and organizational interactions.

- *Participants often hide information from each other.* Information is power in competitive negotiations, and adroit negotiators limit how much they give and try to increase how much they can elicit from the other. Often the participants will distort their intentions, their resources, and their goals with the intent of disguising what they aim to achieve. Some people even feign ignorance or stupidity, since, "In negotiation, dumb is often better than smart, inarticulate better than articulate, and many times weaknesses may actually be strengths (Cohen, 1980, p. 40)." After all, this view asserts, it's easier to achieve a desired goal if the other party doesn't know what it is.

- *Competitive negotiations are often represented by confrontations, arguments, and threats.* Since the relationship between the participants is a low priority, both feel more free to be aggressive. That increases the propensity for arguments and verbal confrontations.

- *The ultimatum is the final ploy.* Tough competitive negotiations often culminate in one party making a "take it or leave it offer." Some participants use this approach inappropriately, though. Once made, it has to be adhered to; you must be willing to walk away from the table if the other side chooses to reject the offer. For that reason, it should only come at the end of the negotiation process, not early on. When it does come, the words used should never belittle the other participant. And, it should provide the other side with a viable alternative; if acceptance of your offer would cause them a loss of face, then both sides are likely to lose this negotiation.

Despite the frequency with which it is used in modern society, competitive negotiations have numerous disadvantages. They produce a strong impetus for confrontation and encourage brinkmanship. The outcomes of competitive negotiations are also harder to predict, particularly if the negotiations become heated; individuals can behave in unexpected ways if anger is aroused or they are threatened with a loss of face. Finally, at least one participant is nearly always disappointed with the results of a competitive negotiation. Frequently, both are. Both parties will tend to enter the negotiation with exaggerated expectations of what to expect, leaving both disappointed when a realistic solution is attained.

Collaborative Negotiation offers a more optimistic view of the negotiation process. It aims for a "win-win" approach with the intent of achieving mutual satisfaction for both parties. As Cohen (1980) noted, "You can get what you want if you recognize that each person is unique and needs can be reconciled. At the same time, never forget that most needs can be fulfilled by the way you act and behave. Mutual satisfaction should be your goal and the means of achievement" (p. 205). In collaborative negotiation, the participants assume that they have some diverse interests, but common interests are also deemed feasible and these are sought. The goal is a mutually agreeable solution that is reached by engaging in a system of joint distribution of resources.

Collaboration Tactics

Collaborative negotiation encompasses a philosophy or mind-set, as much as a set of techniques. As a result, collaborative negotiations can be identified by what communication patterns emerge rather than those that are planned. Wilmot and Hocker (2000) identify five different patterns that are often found in such transactions—(1) Expanding the pie, (2) Payoffs, (3) Logrolling, (4) Cost Cutting, and (5) Bridging. *Expanding the pie* means that both participants look for solutions which satisfy both parties. *Payoffs* are a process in which one party looks for a way to provide some form of compensation to the other party. *Logrolling* is a process of trading off issue priorities by each party. *Cost cutting* occurs when one party looks for ways to minimize the cost of the negotiation to the other party. *Bridging* refers to the invention of new options that meet the others' needs.

Still, some specific tactics are often observed in collaborative groups, including the following:

- *A focus on joint actions.* Collaborative negotiations are characterized by the frequent use of "We" instead of "You" and "I." Participants seek common interests, consult with the other parties before acting, encourage others to speak, and use language that will encourage joint action.

- *A focus on the process.* Collaborative negotiators are more concerned with controlling the negotiation process than with controlling the other person. No attempt is made to sabotage the process. Instead, participation is encouraged, and numerous factors surrounding the process (e.g., setting, timing, number of participants) are analyzed in terms of whether they help or hurt the process. Suggestions for changes are aimed at the process, not the participants.

- *Firm goals, flexible means.* The altruistic assumptions behind collaborative negotiations do not mean that a participant must give up goals in order to please the other participant. Quite the contrary—collaborative negotiators are encouraged to hold firm in their goals, but merely to be flexible in the means they would accept in attaining those goals. The aim should be to stand up for your position without provoking the other person (Ury, 1993). If that mentality can be maintained, then all of the participants can seek alternative means for achieving joint goals.

- *Tackle easy issues first.* Collaborative negotiators assume that there will be a solution reached which will satisfy all the parties, but they recognize that such a solution may not be obtained easily or quickly. To counter that, they address easy issues first. Once those are resolved, that go after the next one—one issue at a time. The success of achieving the first goals will increase optimism for achieving the others.

Characteristics of Collaborative Negotiation

Fisher and Ury (1983) call this form of discussion "Principled Negotiations." They identified four characteristics of such transactions that were related to (1) people, (2) interests, (3) options, and (4) criteria. The "People" component of principled negotiation involves two components. First, the principled negotiator separates the people from the problem, making no attempt to tie judgmental aspects of the those involved to the positions they hold. Second, the "People" component assumes that preserving the relationship between the parties is the primary goal. That generates a reverse mentality on the part of the negotiators. Instead of thinking, "What do I want out of this?," the principled negotiator asks, "What do they want out of this?"

The "Interest" Component emphasizes a need to focus on the interests of other participants, not their positions on the issues. Focusing on issues is more likely trigger a contest of wills. Focusing on interests is more likely to trigger need and goal satisfaction.

Focusing on Interests can also influence the third characteristics—"Options." A contest of wills is likely to degenerate into an argument over only two options—yours and theirs. Collaborative negotiators generate multiple options, a variety of possibilities, before making a decision. Choosing from multiple options, instead of just two, increases the chances of making a better decision.

For that decision to be a quality one, though, the "Criteria" component is critical. The Criteria component of principled negotiations requires that the results of the decision be based on some objective standard. That concept is a natural extension of removing judgmental personal elements from the process. If this can be achieved, all parties will be willing participants in the ultimate decision.

Disadvantages of Collaborative Negotiations

Given the rosy picture painted by scholars, collaborative negotiation has its disadvantages. Perhaps the most important is that—to be most effective—it requires the participation of all parties involved. For that reason, it is relatively easy for a single saboteur to disrupt the process and prevent a reasonable resolution to the problem. Second, the collaborative process can generate strong pressures to accommodate, creating a negotiation-related behavior that is somewhat comparable to "groupthink." Participants may feel pressured to concede too much, giving up things which are in the best interest of their group, and defeating the purpose of the collaborative process.

And third, collaborative negotiations have limited utility in the presence of truly scarce resources. A key assumption behind the process is that options can be expanded so that everyone's needs can be met. In some situations, though, that assumption is simply not available. Such a situation often occurs when working with a limited amount of financial resources, for example, and expanding the pie is an unrealistic option. In those situations, the best available option is a compromise, one in which neither party gets all of what they want. Even that can be a problem if the compromise is the result of third-party negotiations. For example, suppose that labor union representatives meet with management to discuss a possible ten percent pay increase for the workers. Assume also that management believes its workers need a pay increase, but they do not feel that the company can afford a ten percent raise. As a result of the negotiation, in which the union representatives are allowed to examine the financial position of the company, the union negotiators agree and agreement is reached on a compromise raise of five percent. When the union negotiators return to the workers with the offer, the union members may be disappointed. Since they were not directly involved in the negotiation, they will not understand the reason for the compromise. Collaboration efforts led to disappointment, and that could create long term problems for the company.

Telephone Negotiations

Cohen (1980) noted that an increasing number of business-related negotiations occur over the telephone, a medium which requires some adjustments in use of negotiation skills. Several factors contribute to the difference. First, the lack of visual feedback increases the possibility of misunderstanding; participants in telephone negotiations must listen more carefully and rely on more questions and other verbal cues for clarification of ideas and offers. Second, the negotiation "session" is usually brief, particularly when compared to face-to-face meetings; the implied brevity of the phone conversation makes it harder to ask questions, even though more questions are needed. Further, the hurried pace of the phone session increases the risk factor; hasty decisions are often bad decisions, or as Cohen noted, "quick is always synonymous with risk" (p. 212). Third, people generally find it easier to say "no" over the phone than in person; that phenomenon intensifies competitive behaviors over the phone and makes it harder to reach a collaborative agreement over the telephone.

In any telephone negotiation, the advantage goes to the person placing the call, particularly when the call is unexpected. The recipient of an unexpected incoming call is handicapped by a lack of time to prepare, a lack of understanding on the purpose of the call, and no time to consider alternatives. For that reason, Cohen recommends that recipients who are caught off guard should make a graceful exit from the conversation before the negotiations go too far. "Can I call you back in a few minutes" is a reasonable request that gives the recipient time to consider the situation.

Once both parties are on the phone, listening becomes a crucial skill. Successful telephone negotiations require self-discipline to pick up the nuances in verbal messages. These nuances should spark questions which lead to further clarification. The wise telephone negotiator also takes notes, a technique that enhances listening skills while providing a record of the call. In critical negotiations, those notes can be converted into a memo which summarizes the agreement reached between the parties. In fact, all telephone negotiations should be followed by written memos of agreement. As with the initial telephone call, the source of the message has the advantage. The person who writes the memo of agreement can phrase the agreement in the terms that were meaningful to them, rather than the other person.

Dealing with Antagonistic Negotiators

Despite your best efforts, you will still run into a few antagonistic negotiators—verbal pit bulls who insist on attacking you and defeating you personally. Such a person will become an "emotional adversary" who "disagrees with you as a human being" (Cohen, 1983, p. 189). When that occurs, three guidelines apply. First, never forget the power that your attitude has on the negotiation. A collaborative attitude on the part of any one person engenders a similar response from the other. Second, try not to judge the actions and motives of the other person. Their negative attitude may be due to an outside problem unrelated to the negotiation and may dissipate over time. Third, if all else fails, try to avoid the negotiation. There is nothing to be gained by either side if an antagonistic attitude is developed. Breaking off negotiations increases the time pressure for the other party, and the time to cool off may produce better judgments or, in some cases, the selection of a new negotiator by the representatives of the other side.

Summary

Negotiation skills are becoming increasingly important in today's organizational world. The effective negotiator plans for negotiation by (1) gathering information and (2) considering the needs of the other person. Negotiation game plans should include (1) arguments supported by information, (2) trade-offs to be offered, and (3) trust building. The goal should be a collaborative solution, one which meets the needs and desires of both parties.

References

Acuff, F. L. (1997). *How to negotiate anything with anyone, anywhere around the globe.* Chicago: Amacom

Cohen, H. (1980). *You can negotiate anything.* New York: Bantam.

Fisher, R., & Ury, W. (1983). *Getting to yes.* New York: Penguin.

Fuller, G. T. (1991). *The negotiation handbook.* Upper Saddle River, NJ: Prentice-Hall.

McCormack, M. H. (1988). *What they don't teach you at Harvard Business School.* New York: Bantam.

Ury, W. (1993). *Getting past no: Negotiating your way from confrontation to cooperation.* New York: Bantam.

Wilmot, W. W., & Hocker, J. L. (2000). *Interpersonal conflict.* New York: McGraw-Hill

SOMETHING TO THINK ABOUT
PURCHASING A NEW VEHICLE

Assume that your organization has decided to purchase a van to transport group members to local and national meetings. Consider what steps you should consider in preparing and conducting the resulting sales negotiation.

1. What are the needs of the organization, i.e., how many people do you need to transport and how often will it be used?

2. What type of research on the potential vehicle(s) should be done? How much should you expect to pay?

3. Several potential vans may fit your needs. How would you rank them in terms of preference?

4. What dealerships in the area offer the vehicles that interest you? What can you learn about each of them?

5. How can you negotiate with the sales person for the best possible (yet still fair) price? Remember that in collaborative negotiation that you want a good deal, but the sales person also deserves a reasonable profit.

CHAPTER 6

DEALING WITH CONFLICT IN GROUPS

Sally and Bill had worked for the same company for five years. Both worked hard and did their jobs well, as long as they worked separately. Trouble arose, though, when they were placed in a group environment. The problem was that Bill loved to argue, and a group meeting provided him an opportunity to do that. Sally hated arguments and often went out of her way to avoid them. As the group discussion progressed, Sally became increasingly irritated with Bill for antagonizing the group. Similarly, Bill grew increasingly agitated toward Sally's reluctance to enter the fray.

The problem in this situation is that Sally and Bill take two different approaches to handling a major aspect of group communication—conflict. Sally takes a negative view of conflict. She grew up in a home where her father was verbally abusive to her mother. For her, conflict represents a breakdown in communication. As such, it is an unhealthy form of group communication that should be avoided, because it leads to bruised egos and an increased level of tension that is personally uncomfortable. Bill has a positive view of conflict, treating it more like a game. He grew up in a home where his parents encouraged an open debate of issues. For him, conflict is a positive force that stimulates group discussion and allows the group to identify weaknesses in decisions before they are implemented.

These two perspectives represent the difficulty of dealing with conflict in groups. Different people have different perspectives about

the role and utility of conflict in group discussions, and those differences make it difficult for any group to approach conflict in a consistent manner. Still, conflict must be faced within groups if the group
is to have any long term success. With that in mind, though, some
parameters can be established for understanding how conflict operates in groups and how it can be managed. To do that, this chapter
will make the following assumptions.

1. Conflict is neither positive nor negative in nature.
Conflict can exhibit both positive and negative aspects within the
same group, and often does so, but conflict does not inherently deserve either connotation. Whether the outcome of conflict is positive
or negative depends largely upon how the group participants handle
the conflict process.

2. Conflict is normal. We reject the contention that conflict is
an abnormal form of communication that represents a breakdown in
the communication process. Rather, conflict is a normal part of the
communication process that results from differences in personalities
and perceptions. Ignoring those differences is abnormal and hinders
the process.

3. In many cases, conflict cannot and should not **be**
avoided. Quite the contrary, sometimes escalation of conflict is
necessary to resolve the conflict in the long run. Further,
intensification of the controversy can be productive, for it will allow
all issues to be placed on the agenda for discussion. Such process are
not necessarily polite and orderly. In fact, they can be both chaotic
and confusing. But out of the chaos can come productive responses.

4. There is no right way to resolve conflict. Sorry, but you
won't get any easy answers for managing conflict. Conflict is a complicated phenomenon, and the "best" way to resolve or manage it
depends upon the situation and the people involved. All that we can
do is provide some insight and understanding to help you diagnose
each situation.

5. Conflicts differ by types and intensity. A civil discussion
between two colleagues is a productive form of conflict, but one that
operates at a low level of tension. But, if that discussion is repetitive
in nature—i.e., **deja vu conflict,** or one that occurs at regular meetings on an on-going basis—it may represent a deeper form of hostility that must be addressed. Similarly, **mock conflict** (a form of playful interaction between participants) often serves as a positive bond-
ing agent for colleagues. However, if the jokes between the partici-

pants descend to the level of sarcastic sniping, then it can have a strong negative influence on the relationship. Maintaining an effective balance of intensity is key to successful conflict management, regardless of which type is employed.

Defining Conflict

Most people believe they can identify conflict when it occurs, but tacking a precise definition to it can often be confusing. Wilmot and Hocker (2000) perhaps came close when they defined conflict as "an expressed struggle between at least two interdependent parties who perceive incompatible goals, scarce resources, and interference from others in achieving their goals" (p. 3). This definition identifies several key elements that must be present before a particular interaction is considered a conflict.

1. *An expressed struggle.* Jane often told her husband that she disagreed with her boss on some issues. The way she expressed her disagreement, she said, was to remain silent because "that lets him know that I don't agree with him." Not really. That behavior is the avoidance of conflict, not the instigation of it. It may represent hostility or lack of respect, but not conflict. For conflict to be present in a group, the struggle over ideas must be expressed by both parties involved.

2. *Interdependence.* A co-worker and I disagree on political philosophies, and we sometimes express that disagreement. Our disagreement, though, is just that—a disagreement, or difference of opinion, but not a conflict. One element that prevents it from escalating into a conflict is that this particular issue involves no mutual dependence. Which political party controls the executive or legislative branches of government has no direct impact on each of us or our relationship. If we disagreed on hiring a new member of our organization, though, conflict would be present because interdependence would be present. Both of us, working for the same organization, would be affected by the addition of a new worker. How that person would interact, the duties that they would perform, and their relationship with other workers would be a factor that could influence both of us. Interdependence would be present, and so would the potential for conflict.

3. *Incompatible goals.* Interdependence alone does not create conflict. There must be a perception on the part of both parties that the achievement of the goals by one party will prevent the other

party from achieving their goals. This can occur in two manners. First, the parties may have two distinct goals that are incompatible. For example, the department has a chance to hire one additional person, but the current personnel disagree as to what role that person should fulfill. The marketing division wants a new marketing expert, while the sales division believes a new salesperson in most important. The two parties have different goals that are incompatible with each other. Second, the parties may have the same goal, but only one of them can attain that goal. For example, Jane and Bill may both be under consideration for promotion to department chairman, but only one person will receive that promotion. The selection of one person to fill the position will mean that the other will not get the promotion—a situation of incompatible goals.

4. **Scarce Resources.** The second example of incompatible goals also points to another essential element of group conflict—the perception of a shortage of resources. If every party has enough resources to meet their needs, there is rarely any reason for conflict. However, that situation rarely occurs in the modern world. Rather, the scarce-resource variable is often a major problem among work groups, with the organization having insufficient resources to fulfill the goals of every organizational member. Much of the in-fighting among organizations, for example, occurs as various groups within the organization fight over the limited resources available to them. The more limited the resources, the more intense the fighting—a situation that leads to the paradox of people with the least to fight about often fighting the most intensely. Or, as one pundit noted about his organization, "The reason they fight so hard is because there's so little to fight over."

5. **Interference from others.** All of the above conditions could be present, and yet conflict might still be absent. Instead, one additional factor—interference—must also be present. Even in the presence of scarce resources, conflict will occur only if one party interferes with another's efforts to get part of those resources. It is the perception of interference which serves as the final trigger for conflict.

Destructive vs. Constructive Conflict

One factor which contributes to the negative image of conflict is that much of it can be destructive in nature. **Destructive conflicts** are often represented by several characteristics. They may include *deja vu* conflicts, with both parties bringing up the same arguments again and again. They frequently include escalatory spirals in which a minor infraction triggers a series of increasingly hostile responses from both parties. The aftermath of both *deja vu* conflict and escalatory spirals is often a reduction in direct interaction, something done by both parties to avoid or reduce the conflict. But, that results in no resolution until something triggers another round of arguments. Consequently, parties tend to harbor resentment toward each other, make moves that reduce their interdependence, and shift their communication target by complaining to a third person. Retaliation becomes a primary strategy, with both parties seeking to gain a position of one-upmanship. Positions become hardened and inflexible. Verbal messages focus less on issue arguments and more on personal putdowns that are demeaning and degrading to the other person.

Constructive conflict has the opposite characteristics. Constructive conflict enhances self-esteem rather than demeaning individuals. Instead of rigid and inflexible positions, all participants have a willingness to change and a willingness to cooperate. The participants interact with an intent to learn instead of an intent to protect their position. They focus on maintaining the relationship within the group rather than on their individual position within the group. Participants in constructive conflict feel free to express strong feelings, but they do so appropriately; they don't make personal attacks on other parties or the issues under discussion. Constructive conflict does not view the discussion as a zero-sum, win-lose proposition; the discussion process is not one of competition, but one of cooperation. It is a remarkably effective mentality that can produce dramatic results.

Conflict Goals

Wilmot and Hocker (2000) argue that all conflicts are based upon the parties' perceptions of incompatible goals. Effective management of conflict thus depends upon the ability of the parties to have a clear understanding of the goals and objectives for each party involved in the conflict. That may not be as easy as it seems, because conflict goals can operate on multiple levels simultaneously. Managing conflict requires an ability to manage conflict on those multiple goals. Similarly, destructive conflict is limited if all group members have a clear understanding of the group's goals.

Types of Goals

One factor complicating the conflict process is that goals vary in terms of types or dimensions. Specifically, goals operate on at least three dimensions—process, issues, and egos—that can be abbreviated as "P.I.E." goals.

Process Goals

Process goals refers to agreement on what communication processes will be used to decide an issue. Will the group require consensus or majority vote? Will votes be by secret ballot, a show of hands, or voice vote? How will dissident views be expressed—openly or through anonymous postings? Will the decision be made immediately after the discussion, or will the participants have time to consider the options before making a final choice? Such questions relate to how the conflict will be resolve. If these issues are not addressed early in the discussion, those who feel like their side "lost" will argue that they didn't like the process used to make the decision. That leaves them unenthusiastic in their support of the final program.

Issue Goals

Wilmot and Hocker (2000) discuss these in terms of "Content Goals," but under either label it refers to the issue under discussion. Different participants develop different positions on what to do, which decisions are preferable, and how the group's resources should be allocated. This is the surface element of most group conflicts. For the discussion to progress with minimal destructive conflict, these goals should be articulated as precisely as possible. Wilmot and Hocker argued that solutions may come up during the discussion, but they will not be recognized as good ideas if the group doesn't know what it wants. Further, precise goals can be shared with others, redefined more easily and reached in a more straightforward manner. If you know where you're going, it's easier to get there.

Issue goals can vary on the bases of four distinctive factors—facts, values, interests, and side issues. *Facts-based issue conflicts* are disagreements over questions of facts. They typically involve differences in either judgments or perceptions of facts related to the primary conflict issue. *Values-based issue conflicts* are disagreements over the criteria for a decision, with the disagreements representing the articulation of differing values as to what should or should not be the basis for resolving the conflict. *Interest-based issue conflicts* are disagreements over who will get what resources; such issues can be a major source of conflict in work organizations. Finally, *side issues* refer to secondary issues that may be raised by some group members; sometimes these are trivial in nature and merely raised for ego reasons or as a strategic move to distract the group from discussing another issue. Still, some side issues later emerge as major problems, and they should not be automatically dismissed unless the trivial nature of the issue is recognized by all group members.

Ego Goals

Ego, or "face-saving," goals tend to be an underlying tension within group conflicts. Some apparent issue arguments are really face-saving strategies, i.e., verbal messages used by a participant as a means of protecting their ego on some other factor. A group member may object to the allocation of resources for one project, for example, not on the basis of merit but because their own project was not accepted the previous time such an issue was discussed. Ego goals can be influenced by several elements within the group, but two factors tend to dominate: (1) members' self concept and (2) their role within the group. A psychological threat to a member's self concept will almost automatically lead to facework, or face-saving behavior. Face-saving can be such a strong motivator that it often explains the otherwise irrational behavior of a group member. When the ego is threatened, a person will often take dramatic (and sometimes strange) actions to protect it. That will include a refusal to compromise and refusing to step back from an position on an issue.

Closely related to self-concept is the individual's role within the group. How do they define their importance to the group, and how much are they willing to contribute to the group's efforts. If a person feels they have no major role, they will give no major effort. Conversely, highly involved members view the group's goal as important to both the group and to themselves, and their contributions will be significant. They by-product of this is that group conflict can be minimized by a leader who effectively uses techniques that allow members to save or restore face. The authors remember one class incident in which a power struggle between two potential leaders was resolved when one was elected president of the group. The newly elected president's first move was to appoint the losing candidate as second-in-command, asking them to take on many of the powers they were initially seeking. That face-saving move worked to the benefit of both leaders and to the group.

The Variable Nature of Goals. Adding to the complexity of conflict goals is the fact that goals are often in a state of flux—for both the individual and the group. Even if a group leader has a good understanding of the goals of each individual member, there is no guarantee that perception will be valid for long. What individuals want from the group, and what they expect the group to achieve, will often vary—sometimes on a daily basis. At a minimal level, those goals are likely to go through three distinct transformations—an initial goal, a re-evaluation, and a retrospective goal. The initial goal represents what the individual wants out of the group prior to any discussion or conflict. Once the discussion begins, each participant re-evaluates that goal based upon the content of the discussion; objections from some other group members will be strong enough that some of their initial goals will be unattainable, and adjustments are made in priorities so that the focus is shifted to other areas. Once a decision is made, the individual can look back on the discussion and transform their goals again on the basis of a retrospective analysis. They may not have achieved all that they sought, but they are likely to increase the value of those points that were achieved.

Power

Power is discussed in more detail in the chapters on Interpersonal Dynamics and Leadership, but it also plays a critical role in group conflict. Power represents the capacity of an individual to influence their own circumstances. Such influence is essential for conflict; where there is no influence, there is no conflict but merely an exchange of mutual monologues.

Power is a property of the social relationship, not merely a quality of the individual. A person has power over you to the extent that you believe the person has that power. More specifically, your belief in their power is like to be based on your perception of their (1) ability to influence goals that are important to you, and (2) the availability of other avenues of achieving those goals. If Person A has the ability to influence Goal B, and they are the only person who can influence that goal on your behalf, then they have power.

The role of power in conflict is most apparent when there is a power imbalance. The perception that another participant has more power than you can lead to a number of unattractive behaviors. The high power person may acquire a taste for power, viewing the attainment of power as a goal into itself. They may be tempted to abuse their power by improperly using organizational resources for their own personal gain. Pride in their status may create the *Snob Phenomenon*, with the high power person devaluing the less power and avoiding social contact with them. That behavior tends to generate, in turn, false feedback of their worth from subordinates—a response which may intensify the Snob Phenomenon.

Low power individuals are also susceptible to negative behaviors. The immediate response can be a lowered self-esteem that threatens the ego. If they perceive that they lack the power to use legitimate means to attain their goals, they may resort to underhanded tactics to achieve their goals. As a last resort, they may either break off the conflict without resolution or resort to violence as a means of balancing the power.

Because of such precarious effects, the person in the high power position must bear most of the responsibility for a productive use of power. Wilmot and Hocker (2000) calls this approach "the power of calm persistence," and it can be an effective mean of mediating group conflict. The first requirement is that they use their power with restraint. Although a high power source may have a number of options available to use, the overuse of any of those can build up resentment among the low power members. Instead, conflict can be mediated if the high power source remembers the need to focus on the interdependence of the group and its members. That involves a willingness on the part of the high-power person to share some of that power with the low-power members.

Conflict Styles

Conflict styles are the patterned responses or clusters of behavior which people use in conflict. It is a type of conflict behavior which reflects the communication orientations of individuals toward conflict.

Most researchers view conflict styles as a property of the individual group member. That view, in essence, considers conflict style as something akin to a personality type. Even if conflict styles are not indicative of personality, people often get "frozen" into a conflict style. It may be one defined by their gender, with men frequently adopting a competitive style. Others will select a style which they used successfully during the "golden age," a time when they felt best about themselves.

Other researchers assume that many, if not all, individuals can use multiple styles. This view assumes that group members evaluate each conflict situation individually, adopting the conflict style which they believe will be most applicable to the situation. Such adaptability increases the effectiveness of communication by participants and increases their sensitivity to other opinions. Typically, when faced with a conflict in the group, each individual group member is faced with the decision as to whether to engage or not engage in the conflict. Their response to that initial question will influence their choice of conflict style. And still others believe conflict styles represent traits of the individuals, with people choosing to use styles which are reflective of their personality.

Researchers also disagree on the number of stylistic options available to conflict participants—with some arguing for five distinct categories while others limit the options to three. At the very least, though, two options are available to every conflict participant. When placed into a potential conflict situation, the first choice that a person must make is whether to engage or not engage. At the very least then, every person should be capable of handling two distinctly different conflict styles. How they handle them, though, can vary.

Non-Engagement Conflict Styles

Conflict participants have two stylistic options if they choose not to engage in conflict. They can choose to (1) avoid the conflict, or (2) accommodate the other person.

Avoidance. Sometimes the easiest way to resolve a conflict is simply to avoid it. Most people, when faced with a triggering event, make a quick assessment as to whether that event is something "worth fighting about." If not, they mentally shrug their shoulders and avoid the conflict.

The Avoidance style is the purest form of non-engagement. People who prefer the avoidance style will sometimes take extreme measures to avoid any active conflict whatsoever. The avoidance style is characterized by such tactics as denial of conflict, equivocation, changing and avoiding topics, being non-committal, irreverent comments, and using joking as a way not to deal with the conflict at hand.

People who use the avoidance style have a number of tactics at their disposal. That can, for example, deny the existence of any conflict ("I'm not upset about anything), evasive remarks ("What are you talking about?"), change or avoid the topic, take a non-committal position, or use jokes as a way to avoid the conflict. On minor issues, this is a highly effective technique by helping to promote harmony and keeping people from getting unnecessarily upset.

Avoiding conflict does not prevent it, and continued avoidance of a long-term problem can be highly destructive by letting the conflict build up to more intense levels. Further, avoidance can lower the members satisfaction with the group in general, creating other long-term problems and undermining the member goals of the group. Still, some potential conflicts are so minor that they are hardly worth fighting over. Avoidance of such minor conflicts help to promote harmony and keep group members from getting unnecessarily upset.

On bigger issues, in particular, avoidance merely prolongs or delays the conflict. Participants who feel forced to avoid conflict on major issues generally feel more stress and grow increasingly dissatisfied with their situation. When the eventual conflict does occur, it can be highly destructive in nature. It can lead to unhappy relationships, whether in a marriage or at work, if it keeps important issues buried.

Accommodation. One easy way to avoid conflict is to simply accommodate the desires of the other person, or simply "Tolerate it." The Accommodation Style of conflict management is a non-assertive form of non-engagement, one in which the individual group member allows the wishes of another group member to dominate. The technique, in its simplest form, is to simply give up or give in to the other person's demands. Others engage in accommodation by denying their own needs ("It's not important to me") or expressing a desire for harmony ("I just want to be sure everybody's happy").

Individuals who prefer the accommodation style put high values on cooperation and harmony within the group. This approach has the advantage of maintaining group harmony with the presence of any overt conflict. Participants who use this style are generally viewed as being "reasonable" by other group members, and it thus limits the likelihood that you will become the target of any personal sabotage.

Such an approach has its advantages. It's a particularly effective technique when you realize you're wrong. Shifting to an accommodation approach at that point demonstrates that you're a reasonable person. It's also an effective means of maintaining harmony within a relationship without engaging in overt conflict. Further, in dangerous situations, it can be a means of keeping other people from harming you. When facing an armed robber who has demanded "Your money or your life," accommodation is the wisest course of action.

However, accommodation does have its limitations. In any specific instance, it may simply be a pseudo-solution that hides the real problems. Further, accommodation can be particularly ineffective if a person adopts it as their primary conflict style in a relations.

If that occurs, the boundaries of the relationship are never tested; instead, a power imbalance is created that is intensified each time accommodation behavior is used. Consequently, other group members might eventually interpret constant accommodation as an indicator of lack of commitment to the group. For the group as a whole, it can sometimes lead to a pseudo-solution in which group members falsely assume that consensus has been achieved.

Engagement Styles of Conflict

If a group member chooses to engage another member in conflict, they have three basic conflict styles to choose from: Competition, Compromise, or Collaboration.

Competition. The competitive approach is characterized by assertive or aggressive attitudes and "win-lose" tactics in which the individual pursues their own concerns at the expense of the other people involved in the situation. Competitive behavior is not necessarily bad. An individual can pursue their interests in an assertive manner without taking advantage of other people. Sometimes such assertive behavior is necessary to exercise one's rights in a democracy. Such behavior is particularly important if the issue itself is important; your assertiveness demonstrates your commitment to the principle.

At its basic level, the primary tactic of competition is argumentation. In terms of achieving what they want individually, group members who prefer the competitive style have a competitive edge over those members who prefer to avoid or accommodate. On the positive side, competitive conflict demonstrates commitment to an issue and can lead to quick and decisive results. On the negative side, it can harm relationships within the group by not accounting for individual goals among other group members, particularly in terms of their needs to save face.

In addition, individuals who do not assert themselves in some situations are viewed as "pushovers." The catch is to be assertive without being aggressive, i.e., asserting your own rights without berating or ridiculing the other person. That can be hard to do. Once the competitive mode is engaged, it's easy to slip into a strategic model in which you try to build up your position by cutting down the other person. When that occurs, competition has gone too far. The signs are easy to spot. Instead of discussing issues, the topic of conversation shifts to personal criticism, hostility, and denial of responsibility.

Compromise. Compromise is the intermediate style, a give-and-take process in which both participants win a little and both lose a little. This "meeting in the middle" approach is a tried-and-true approach to solving difficult problems. It is often the "last ditch" effort used by groups when all other approaches have failed. In that situation, it usually works well. However, as a long-term approach to resolving conflicts, compromise is over-rated. While it guarantees that both parties will win something, it also ensures that both will lose something. It is an effective back-up method, working best when other styles and techniques have failed. It can lead to a group decision with relatively little expenditure in time, and serves to save face for group members by reinforcing an equal distribution of power. Generally, most group members like the concept of compromise, viewing it as a "morally correct" and "fair" means of achieving group goals.

However, it can become an easy way out which avoids issues which might need to be discuss, leaving everybody somewhat dissatisfied with the proposed solution. While this can be tolerated in some instances, extended use of this approach tends to build up resentment. Further, the resulting decision may leave everybody disappointed. Derisive comments that a camel is "a horse built by a committee" typically refer to the awkward elements of decisions that come out of hasty compromises. Use it when you need to, but don't overuse it.

Collaboration. Collaboration is the "ideal" conflict style, one in which all conflict participants work toward an ideal solution which will satisfy all of the individual and group goals. Collaboration places a heavy requirement on the use of such tactics as analytical remarks, descriptive statements and conciliatory remarks. When successful, collaborative solutions tend to generate new ideas that satisfy all group members. It has the added value of showing respect for the individual members while gaining.

The collaboration approach aims for win-win solutions, i.e., pleasing everybody involved. Realistically, that cannot always be achieved. Pragmatically, though, such an ideal can be achieved far more often than many participants may realize. The catch is to be open-minded and willing to look at additional alternatives– not just those represented by the different sides of the conflict. This is the ideal approach for long-term relationship. It shows respect for each participant and results in strong commitment from all of the parties.

The disadvantage is that its success depends upon the generation of new ideas, and that process is typically time-consuming. Creative solutions don't come quickly or easily. This requires more work and more effort on the part of all participants. Arguments are presented as descriptive statements, with no evaluative connotations. Individuals are treated with respect.

Collaboration can also be highly time-consuming and tiring. Further, high power sources can sometimes manipulate the process through a technique known as pseudo-collaboration, leading the group to a pre-determined solution.

Regardless, collaboration often works. But, given the fact that many group participants enter a meeting with the desire to keep it as short as possible, there is always a tension within the group to avoid the collaborative approach. Other approaches are quicker and easier. When you're tired of talking and meeting, you may take the easy approach—even if it's the wrong approach.

The Self Regulation of Anger

Anger and hostility are the predominate emotions associated with conflict interactions. Anger can be viewed as the feeling connected to a perceived unfairness or injustice. Ancient philosophers described it as "the moral emotion" because it is often based on reflective judgment. Despite the widespread recognition of anger, it is not a primary emotion. Wilmot and Hocker (2000) describe it as a secondary emotion, and many other emotions often accompany it—particularly alienation and powerlessness. The interference stage of conflict triggering seems to play a major role, since anger is often based on the frustration of unmet needs and desires.

Anger can be manifested in four different ways. We can be angry with others, angry at ourselves, angry about something from the past (usually of an on-going nature), or angry at life. The latter, also known as abstract anger, is more commonly referred to as the "chip on the shoulder." In either form, its presence is literally controversial. Psychologists still debate whether anger is a healthy or harmful emotion. One common argument is that the expression of anger is a healthy form of catharsis that allows for the ventilation of emotion. There seems to be some truth to both points, depending upon how the anger is expressed. Here are four guidelines for the responsible expression of anger: (1) Verbally state the anger ("I am angry"), (2) draw distinction between venting and acknowledging anger, (3) agree to never attack in a state of anger, and (4) find the stimulus for the anger.

Others argue that anger is an unhealthy emotion, one that increases the chances of heart problems. One version of the catharsis theory is that acting out your anger helps to relieve tension, but a study at Harvard found the opposite effect; acting out one's anger increases a person's hostility, rather than reducing it (Bushman & Stack, 1999). Also, expressing anger in an unrestrained way simply makes others angry, creating a potential cycle of conflict. Further, every individual has some responsibility to practice some level of self-restraint. Just because you feel angry doesn't mean you have to behave irrationally. To do so can create situations that we will later regret, by increasing the cycle of conflict. In the final analysis, angry behavior rarely solves a problem. It only allows for a venting or catharsis of emotion. When the venting is over, the problem still exists.

Even worse, the anger may not actually be directed at the other person, but at ourselves. Often anger is only indirectly related to the triggering event; instead, most of it is inner-directed. We blame ourselves for feelings of stupidity, embarrassment, lack of control, or powerlessness, and we lash out at somebody else to protect our self-threatened ego.

The other party, of course, has no way of knowing that. People who are the targets of verbal tirades are often caught off guard and respond with anger themselves. When it happens, a more effective technique is to acknowledge the other person's anger, clarify your behavior, and invite them to help you work out a solution. If you maintain an optimistic, relational attitude while doing this, it usually diffuses the initial angry response.

Personality Influences
Some people are more susceptible to anger than others. The three most dominant personality traits with high susceptibility are (1) the volatile personality, (2) the thin-skinned personality, and (3) the alienated individual.

Volatility. Contrary to popular opinion, anger is not a primary emotion. Instead, it is a secondary emotion which is typically triggered by a connection to some perceived unfairness or injustice (Wilmot & Hocker, 2000). Some group members, those who might be called **the volatile personality**, are highly susceptible to anger. They tend to explode at the slightest of injustices, with their anger sometimes leading to violence. Often, such explosions are only dimly related to the precipitating event. Instead, for the volatile personality, most anger is inner-directed: blaming oneself for feelings of stupidity, embarrassment, lack of control, or powerlessness. The anger becomes a way of covering the resulting feeling of inferiority.

The volatile personality tends to have five sub-components or characteristics: (1) aggressiveness, (2) a strong moral code, (3) a hair trigger, (4) an inner misery, and (5) a sense of inferiority. Each of these can be viewed as a required element of the volatile personality. If any single one of these is missing, the individual is unlikely to be considered volatile. Any anger episodes that they might have would likely fall within normal ranges. But, put all five together and you have a potentially lethal mix of personality elements

Aggressiveness is the first component. Despite its negative connotations, aggression is not an inherently negative personality trait. Aggression is a highly valued trait in a number of fields, including the business world and sports. But aggressive tendencies can lead to volatile explosions if mixed with the other four elements.

Second on the list is the presence of a strong moral code. This factor surprises some people, because of the image of volatile personalities as people whose tirades can result in death or injury to others. From their perspective, though, such extreme actions are justified by a sense of injustice that has been incurred by them. They typically view themselves as the victims, justifying their explosive behavior on the basis that the person they attacked "made them do it."

Closely associated with the strong moral code is the presence of a hair trigger. It doesn't take much to make them angry. A strong moral code makes it easier for them to experience that sense of injustice, because even a minor infraction has the potential of being viewed as unjust.

Adding to the mix of volatility is often some form of inner misery. Its nature may vary, but people with volatile personalities typically had abusive childhoods, came from homes with substance abuse problems, or experienced some form of traumatic experience at a younger age.

Such negative experiences as a child perhaps contributes to the final component—a sense of inferiority. Everybody feels inadequate at some time or another, but volatile personalities typically feel this way almost constantly. The presence of a triggering event not only threatens them on an issue level, but it is perceived as a direct threat on their battered ego. They respond, trying to shield their sense of inferiority with anger.

Thin-Skinned Personalities. "Thin-skinned" refers to those people who have trouble accepting criticism. They share many of the personality traits of the volatile personality, particularly the sense of inferiority, but their lack of aggressiveness distinguishes them from the above group. Rather than lashing out in response to others, they withdraw with hurt feelings. Generally, thin-skinned people have three characteristics in common. They (1) take themselves too seriously, (2) avoid accepting responsibility, and (3) have no sense of humor. The second element is barrier to their handling of anger. Dealing with anger requires that a person take responsibility for their own behavior, instead of saying everybody else is over reacting.

Alienation. Alienation is the degree to which an individual believes their behavior can determine the outcomes they seek. An individual experiences alienation whenever they cannot provide themselves with desired rewards, or are unable to avoid negative sanctions. Such a condition is dependent upon at least four characteristics, three identified by Stokols (1975) and the fourth discusssed by Seeman (1959). A state of psychological alienation (1) originates in a social relationship, (2) results from disillusionment with the quality of the relationship, (3) is maintained by spatial or psychological proximity, and (4) is based upon the perceived powerlessness of the individual to restore the situation to its previous positive state.

The first distinctive characteristic of alienation is that it "develops in the context of an on-going relationship between an individual and another person or group of people" (Stokols, 1975, p. 27). That element makes long-term groups a prime source of alienated behavior in that the group itself places an individual into a social environment. The second characteristic of alienation is that it involves a process of disillusionment, i.e., "an unexpected deterioration in the quality of outcomes provided by the individual to the other." In most instances, disillusionment implies the existence of a social relationship which was, at a previous time, satisfactory to the individual and provided them with positive rewards.

The third characteristic of alienation is proximity. Alienation "persists to the extent that the individual and the other(s) remain spatially or psychologically proximal" (Stokols, 1975, p. 27). This proximity serves to constantly remind the individual of their disillusionment. Finally, the fourth distinctive characteristic of alienation is powerlessness, or "the expectancy or probability held by the individual that his own behavior cannot determine the occurrence of the outcomes or reinforcements he seeks." It relates to the perceived capability of an individual to affect his own environment. Powerlessness is important to alienation because it is the key element contributing to frustration. Thus, even though disillusionment creates dissatisfaction, alienation is not experienced until the individual perceives themselves as being unable to correct the situation or to restore the former relationship. If an individual has the power to restore the relationship to its former positive position, the dissatisfaction will be removed and alienation eliminated. If not, frustration will continue and alienation maintained. Anger will be the ultimate outcome.

Alienation can generally be relieved or avoided entirely by ensuring that all group members won't experience a feeling of powerlessness. As long as that element is missing, frustration levels should not be high enough to engender alienation. Again, successful enhancement of the group task will be dependent upon satisfaction of the members' individual goals.

Angry personalities tend to go through a similar sequence in developing anger, one that also tends to describe the anger reactions of most people. First, there is *Trigger*, a situation or statement made by another person. That is followed quickly by a thought ("What did I do to deserve that"), an evaluation ("That's unfair"), and a feeling of hurt or betrayal. Sometimes there is a fantasy about retaliation. Overtly, the volatile personality responds with an explosive reaction—shouting, hitting or breaking objects. The thin-skinned typically adopts other negative behaviors such as pouting or sulking.

Despite the frequency of such responses, most people can learn self restraint if they approach their anger as a problem to be solved. As psychologist Redford Williams (1999) noted, people can be trained to behave differently even if their personality cannot be changed. The general guidelines for self restraint are to evaluate each anger even in terms of importance, justification and intention—Is this situation important to you? Is anger justified in this situation? And is the other person "out to get you"? Simple guidelines for dramatic results. Even if you don't use this particular approach, though, self-restraint is expected in modern society. Without it, conflict escalates too far and everyone suffers.

Stages of Conflict Development and Resolution

Several researchers have attempted to describe how conflict emerges and how it can be controlled. One of these approaches, Stuart's Conflict Containment Stages (Stuart, 1980) divides the typical conflict into six distinctive stages:

1. *Trigger Stage.* The trigger is the event which brings a conflict into mutual awareness. It is identified by the participants' recognition of their first emotional reaction to the conflict issue. Some conflicts

can be deflated at this point by the participant themselves, if they can identify why the triggering event made them angry. Typically, the anger emerges because the trigger represented interference toward achieving some specific goal, regardless of the relative priority of that goal. If the trigger interfered with a relatively minor goal, it may not be worth engaging in conflict to resolve. If it's a major one, the person should at least pause and consider the consequences of escalating the conflict. Sometimes the trigger is a minor part of a longer, on-going conflict. In those instances, it is necessary to understand the nature of the ongoing relationship between the other events in which the trigger is embedded. For *example*, a spouse's comment on cleaning up the house may trigger an argument that actually began days or weeks earlier over shared responsibility of household duties.

2. *Reflex Stage.* The reflex is the response to the trigger, and it is often done in open anger. Because of the emotional nature of the reflex, it can be hard to control—at least initially. Still, how the anger is expressed can have a major impact on the destructive or constructive nature of the conflict. Typically, whether the conflict escalates at this point will depend upon the target of the anger. Was the anger directed at the individual or merely at their action? Was the anger justified, or was it perceived as an over-reaction? Did the reflex include a request for a change on the part of the other person? If so, was the request reasonable and specific? All of these factors can influence the direction of the conflict.

3. *Reflex Fatigue.* The third stage is the reaction of the other party to the expression of reflexive anger. At this point, two things can occur. First, the second party can have their own reflex reaction, becoming angry because the first party became angry. Or, they can identify the anger of the other person and dispel it. That can typically be done by (1) expressing recognition of the other's anger, and (2) asking what you should do in the future.

4. *Commitment Stage.* If the second party is successful in the reflex fatigue stage, the first conflict exchange shifts back to the injured party. If the anger has been dispelled, they are likely to begin a shift of the discussion to a people-based relationship issue. A typical and effective comment by the injured party at this stage is to say, "I'm going to sit and tell you how frustrating this has been for me."

5. *Reconsolidation.* The anger initially resulting from the trigger may be too intense for the participants to resolve the conflict then and there, but progress can be made. At the very least, the partici-

pants can engage the problem and reach an agreement to work on it. That, at least, restores the relational balance between the participants.

6. *Reapproachment.* When the relationship is restored, both participants may be inclined to drop the conflict after the reconsolidation stage. Stuart, however, suggests that time should be taken for one final element. The participants should summarize what they have learned, acknowledging the lesson, and making agreements to change.

Getting Involved in Conflict Resolution

Sometimes group conflict can escalate into unhealthy ranges, and someone must step in to restore the process. While many group members will look to the leader to do that, that may not necessarily work. Sometimes, any attempt by the leader to facilitate conflict resolution is viewed negatively by all sides of the dispute, since any action could be interpreted as "siding" with one of the views. Quite frequently, then, a major part of the responsibility for resolving group conflict rests with the members of the group themselves. What can you, as an individual member, do in such situations?

1. *Start with yourself.* There are three different ways for resolving a group conflict. You can (1) change the other party, (2) change the situation, or (3) change your own behavior. Our egos tend to point us toward the first option—getting the other person to change their position so that it favors ours. That, however, is the hardest of the three options to achieve. Conversely, changing our own behavior is the most successful way to resolve a conflict. It is difficult to do, though, merely because of the ego adjustments that have to be made and the implication that you are admitting defeat on the issue. However, adjusting your own behavior does not require that you necessarily alter an opinion that you believe is correct. It merely requires that you change the antagonistic behavior that triggers negative responses from the other party.

2. *Lower the level of antagonism.* Your goal should not be to eliminate conflict, but merely to lower the level of antagonism to a midrange or moderate level that can be productive. The issues are still available for debate and discussion. Such an action has several positive impacts on the group. It tends to halt the destructive conflict from all parties, because social pressure will prevent the other party from continuing the discussion at an unproductive level. It also releases group energy for productive uses; instead of yelling at each other, the participants can turn their attention to more creative solu-

tions than they had been exploring. Your willingness to lower the antagonism, though, will also bring some positive benefits to you. Typically, the person who first emerges as the peacemaker is viewed positively by the group. It simultaneously allows you to assert yourself as in independent and legitimate party in the debate, while recognizing the mutual dependence of the group members. The result: your credibility is enhanced.

3. *Look at the situation.* Once you have decided to lower your own level of hostility, you are better positioned to look at the situation from a different perspective. Such an attitude creates the possibility of other options that may achieve the goals of more of the participants—not just yours. This aspect doesn't always work, simply because some alternative are mutually exclusive; accepting one means the automatic rejection of another. But the number of mutually exclusive conflicts is much smaller than most participants realize, because their anger and hostility interferes with their ability to consider other alternatives. If that hostility is reduced, the possibility of other mutually acceptable options often emerges.

Another way of dealing with the situation is a process called *fractionation*, or subdividing the conflict issues into smaller, more manageable units. In the heat of conflict fractionation can be difficult to achieve, but it is often a relatively easy process from a slightly more objective viewpoint. If conflicts are broken down into smaller units, resolving the conflicts becomes a simple series of tasks rather than a single insurmountable problem.

4. *Choose a Mechanism.* Even with your own reduction in hostility, the conflict will not naturally resolve itself. Instead, some mechanism must be developed which allows the other participants to reduce their own hostility. That typically requires some group mechanism which allows for either the airing or resolving of grievances. Some organizations schedule regular "Gripe Times" which allow members to express their concerns. Others call special meetings to address specific problems. Or you might use a regularly scheduled meeting as an opportunity to address a current problem. Regardless of which format is chosen, though, some guidelines should be followed if the discussion is to be productive. Wilmot and Hocker (2000) suggest using a Conflict Containment model based upon three basic elements: (1) focusing on the present, not the past, by asking "How" instead of "Why," (2) adopting a conciliatory mind set in which you speak positively about the other party instead of trying to "win" the issue, and (3) seeking solutions in small steps by addressing one issue

at a time. Gorman's guidelines for Practical Crisis Management emphasizes the need to (1) stop the destructive exchanges, (2) be agreeable, even if you feel wronged, and (3) be willing to accept an imperfect solution because imperfect solutions are better than none.

Another option, ABCD Analysis, suggests that the participants analyze the conflict along four dimensions—Antecedents, Behaviors, Consequences, and Do different. Antecedents require a look at the past by identifying what led to the crisis. Behaviors refers to an identification of how each person acted in coping with the situation. Consequences looks at the outcomes of those behaviors both on the individuals and the group. The Do Different stage asks the participants to identify what can be done differently that could alleviate the tension within the group. The goal of this approach is to at least negotiate a temporary agreement that halts the immediate conflict while a long-range solution can be developed.

Outside Intervention

Sometimes group conflict can escalate to the point that the participants feel unable to resolve the problem themselves. In those situations, the group could consider some form of outside intervention to help break the deadlock. Several options are available.

Unstructured Third Party Intervention. Third party intervention can be either a formal or informal process, structured or unstructured in its development. Unstructured intervention can be as informal as talking to a friend or colleague about the problem; that approach allows for articulation of concerns and a source of supportive communication, but may do little to alleviate a problem. At a slightly more formal level, unstructured intervention can include discussing your problem with an immediate supervisor or personnel officer. The supervisor will be positioned to have an inside view of the problem, but is likely to be involved in the problem in some manner; that could hinder impartiality in providing advice. An organizational personnel officer may not understand the conflict as well as a supervisor, but they can offer a more objective view; at the very least, they can determine if the situation needs immediate attention and if additional outside advice (such as an attorney) is needed.

Mediation. Mediation is a process in which an outside person helps the parties change their positions so they can reach agreement. Mediation typically involves a four-step process of (1) establishing an agenda, (2) having the parties exchange information, (3) negotiating the differences, and (4) accepting a resolution that maintains the relationship among the parties. The use of a mediator has the advantage of promoting a mutual stake in the resolution, and its flexibility allows for the introduction of integrative and creative solutions. It works, though, only if all parties agree to cooperate and only if all parties are committed to maintaining the relationship. If those factors are missing, mediation can be a waste of time and effort.

Arbitration. Arbitration occurs when the conflict parties mutually agree to let a third party decide the outcome of the conflict. Two forms are used in the legal system. **Binding arbitration** is a process in which the arbitrator chooses one side or the other, and both parties must abide by the decision. In binding arbitration, there is no compromise position. One position is selected as the winner; the other loses—much like a judge would decide on the guilt or innocence of a person on trial. **Non-binding arbitration** allows for either further arbitration or the right to pursue the case further. It is, in essence, a preliminary discussion of the conflict that allows for the introduction of other viewpoints and the opinion of an outside observer. In either approaches, it can prevent the use of impasse techniques. Still, to be effective, both parties must agree to enter the arbitration, and the arbitrator must be trained in the process.

Consultation. Non-binding arbitration might be considered as a form of consultation. Consultation occurs when the group calls upon the advice and expertise of an outside third party. For example, the authors had a class working on a group project who reached an impasse on how to handle a planned advertising program that was part of the project. Their solution: they asked a representative of a professional advertising agency to sit in on their discussion and give them advice. Through that approach, the parties representing the various sides of the original argument began to recognize the strengths and weaknesses of their individual approaches. The final solution was one that integrated the strengths of both positions.

Summary

Regardless of which approach is taken, conflict intervention is most effective when at least one participant enters the foray with the intention of halting hostilities. When one person initiates a non-hostile action, it frequently triggers a reciprocal action by the other party. Beyond that, the success of the intervention can depend upon several factors. These include:

1. An identification of all the issues. Sometimes you may intervene merely to resolve an issue directly related to you. That issue

may be so tied to other issues, that one cannot be resolved until the others are addressed. When that occurs, the issues must be divided and addressed individually, but the process cannot stop until all issues are addressed.

2. The value of the relationship. The chances of resolving a conflict over any issue increases to the extent that both parties value their relationship to the group. If the group has a short-term existence, or some members feel no allegiance to the group, then the chances of any intervention success is decreased.

3. Timing. One critical skill in the identification process is identify the right time to consider intervention. If you move too quickly, the parties may still be holding a simmering resentment that interferes with resolution. Wait too long and the positions of both parties may become so hardened that resolution is difficult.

4. Power balancing. As noted in a previous chapter, power plays a vital role in an organizational context. Any attempt to resolve conflict with no consideration of power is likely doomed to defeat.

5. Process selection. Informal approaches to resolution should be tried first. Informal processes offer an opportunity for resolution that can potentially provide a face-saving solution to all parties involved. If informal approaches fail, structured resolution techniques may be required. Regardless of which is used—mediation, arbitration, or consultation—it should be one to which all parties agree.

References

Bushman, B. J., & Stack, A. D. (1999). Catharsis, aggression, and persuasive influence: Self-fulfilling or self-defeating prophecies? *Journal of Personality & Social Psychology, 76,* 367-376.

Seeman, M. (1959). On the meaning of alienation. *American Sociological Review, 24,* 783-791.

Stokols, D. (1975). Toward a psychological theory of alienation. *Psychological Review, 82,* 26-44.

Stuart, R. B. (1980). *Helping couples change.* New York: Guilford.

Williams, R. (1999). *Anger kills: Seventeen strategies for controlling the hostility that can harm your health.* New York: HarperTorch.

Wilmot, W. W., & Hocker, J. L. (2000) *Interpersonal conflict.* New York: McGraw-Hill.

A SELF-ADMINISTERED ANGER SCALE

Some researchers used this quiz to rank anger levels of 1,300 people in a study of temper and heart risks. To gauge your "anger ranking," give yourself one point for each "true" answer to Nos. 1-15 and one point for a "false" answer to No. 16.

1. At times I feel like swearing.

2. At times I feel like smashing things.

3. Often I can't understand why I have been so irritable and grouchy.

4. At times I feel like picking a fistfight with someone.

5. I easily become impatient with people.

6. I am often said to be hotheaded.

7. I am often so annoyed when someone tries to get ahead of me in a line of people that I speak to that person about it.

8. I have at times had to be rough with people who were rude or annoying.

9. I am often sorry because I am so irritable and grouchy.

10. It makes me angry to have people hurry me.

11. I am very stubborn.

12. Sometimes I get so angry and upset I don't know what comes over me.

13. I have gotten angry and broken furniture or dishes when I was drinking.

14. I've become so angry with someone that I have felt as if I would explode.

15. I've been so angry at times that I've hurt someone in a physical fight.

16. I almost never lose self-control.

Grades
  0-1: Low
  2-4: Average
  5-14: High

Source:
Bushman, B. J., & Stack, A. D. (1999). Catharsis, aggression, and persuasive influence: Self-fulfilling or self-defeating prophecies? *Journal of Personality & Social Psychology, 76,* 367-376.

SOMETHING TO THINK ABOUT

CONFLICT AND THE RUMOR MILL

The organizational rumor mill (aka, the grapevine) is a major communication force within most groups and also a potential source of conflict. Attempts to control the rumor mill are usually futile. The best you can do is to understand why it works and its effectiveness, and then monitor it within your own group.

Why is it always present? Workers tend to get confusing and/or incomplete messages from their supervisors. In the absence of complete information, the rumor mill helps to fill in the gaps.

How effective is it? Its accuracy is sometimes questionable, but the speed with which it operates isn't. Workers often hear about supervisory decisions before they are officially announced.

Why should you monitor the rumor mill? Because even if the information in it is false, it provides an understanding of member concerns. The issues on the grapevine are the ones that most concern the other group members.

Considering these factors, assume that you've heard a rumor that the personnel in your department will be cut by 25 percent. With only eight workers, that would mean that two people could lose their jobs. What would you do with this information? With whom would you talk and what would you wish to discuss with them?

CHAPTER 7

MONITORING AND EVALUATING BEHAVIOR

The term "monitor" means "to warn." Such warning, though, is dependent on observations. When working within groups there are two types of codes that must be observed in order to know what is *really* going on in the discussion. The codes we use are verbal and nonverbal. When a member sits away from the table, when one refuses to talk, when members joke instead of taking the meeting seriously, when members are doodling, there are observations to be made and ultimately analyses to be created. Sometimes, though, the meanings are not as obvious as one might expect. In this chapter, we will discuss some of the observations that may be made and some methods for analyzing what we observe.

Purposes of Monitoring and Evaluating Behavior
As we have discussed throughout this book, the first purpose of monitoring is to determine whether you and the other group members are "on the same page." In most cases, all of the members will not be on the same page for a variety of reasons. Some want the meeting to last a long time because they would rather meet than go back to their other tasks at hand. Others want the meeting to finish quickly so that they may go back to their tasks at hand. Some feel that group meetings are lacking in purpose—that they resolve nothing. There is a ***clearing process*** that must take place early in each

meeting. This process is a re-negotiation of the relationships among the participants in such a way as to determine the standing of each of the others. Only when members are operating from the same **set of assumptions** is it possible to accomplish anything in the group.

If we take a group of four people who interact each morning before work, playing bridge for an hour we can see some of what we are discussing. Each of the members knows that the purpose is to enjoy the playing of cards. Although work discussion may come into play, it is important that the discussion not interfere with the task at hand—to play bridge. If a player misses a play because of the lack of concentration, it will likely be noted, perhaps even verbally. Often the clearing process is for the purpose of seeing to it that the group members are functioning with the same set of assumptions. If a group member gets up to get coffee several times during the game, such a distraction may lead another to point out that "Aren't we here to play bridge?" While a daily bridge game may not usually be considered a meeting, it may be looked upon as a maintenance meeting—for the purpose of keeping the group together.

How we go about determining whether there is a set of assumptions agreed upon is formulated in two ways—verbally and nonverbally. In the examples previously mentioned, others may say something. They may use verbal communication. But we also make such a determination from nonverbal acts. For example, a player may appear to be especially listless, lacking in concentration, or hurried. The nonverbal gestures that illustrate these feelings have an impact on the other group members. In some cases, the nonverbal actions of one lead to verbal actions on the part of another. Then, someone may say, "Are you okay today?" In the paragraphs that follow, we will look at some of the verbal and nonverbal factors that help us determine whether we are on the same page—whether we are operating out of the same set of assumptions. We begin with the nonverbal.

Observing Nonverbal Behavior

When we enter a meeting room, we tend to observe several factors. One of the significant factors is where people sit. Our traditions tell us that the "leader" sits at the end of the table. It is important when going to a meeting for the first time, that one observe where others are sitting before taking a seat. There are usually practical or historical reasons why people sit where they do. The person next in charge to the leader is likely to be seated at an adjacent seat—researchers generally say to the left of the boss. Our observations indicate, however, that the second person is almost equally likely to sit on the right. In addition, there are often more chairs than there are seats at the table. The outside seats are usually intended for those who are guests—people who may be there for only a few minutes—and for administrative support personnel, who may have to leave the room to obtain additional information. Primary participants tend to sit at the table. If a primary participant does not sit at the table, there is often some historical reason. This participant is unlikely to participate very much. He or she may be apprehensive and shy, or he or she may have some grudge against a member of the group or the group as a whole.

Early in the meeting, too, we note who comes to the meeting first and who comes last. Being late for a meeting occasionally is likely to go unnoticed. However, regular tardiness is noticed and is condemned by the other members of the group. Such behavior shows a lack of respect for the work of the group. Such behavior is rude and is likely to be politically damaging. Of course, the leader can do this because many consider that this is her meeting. The leader has other things to do or may be making last minute preparations. No doubt, then, proxemics (the study of space) and chronemics (the study of time) affect the workings of a group. There are other nonverbal aspects of the human interaction process which affect how well or how poorly groups work. These nonverbal elements include kinesic behavior (gestures, facial expression, eye behavior), physical appearance (body shape, clothing, accessories), haptics (touching behavior), vocalics, and olfaction (the study of smell). As a final element of nonverbal behavior, we will take another look at proxemics, focusing on what should and should not be present at a meeting.

Kinesic Behavior

Most of us are fairly careful about how we gesture while we are working in a meeting. We are careful not to engage in much hand-to-face behavior. We usually do not scratch. We try to keep our eyes open. We try to appear as if we are paying close attention. Certainly it is important to pay attention to our own gestures, but it is just as important to attend what others in the group are doing.

There are seven basic emotions that are typically shown in the facial area: happiness, sadness, fear, anger, disgust, contempt, and surprise. **Happiness** is an emotion that is rarely seen in group meetings. Most people are required to be there. The agenda is fairly formal. It just isn't the place to be happy. However, the extent to which smiles are present in meetings is an indicator of the lack of frustration, somewhat a lack of formality, and a general feeling that spontaneity is appreciated. Happiness may be shown when the leader explains that the group has done a better job than last year and there will be Christmas bonuses for everyone. **Sadness** is another emotion rarely seen in meetings. This is not because there is a lack of happiness in the meeting. Rather it is because the members of the group attempt to "cover up" their feelings of sadness. When a good leader retires or when the good leader is promoted, the other members often feel sad, fearful, and frustrated.

Fear is a common emotion in meetings. Some members fear that they may be asked a question for which they do not know the answer. Some meetings entail discussions of low profits and possible downsizing. When this occurs, those at the table are concerned about their own survival as well as the possibility that they will have to notify one of their subordinates that his services are not needed. *Disgust* is often seen in the faces of people who are tired of hearing the same things. Some may show disgust for particular members of the group, especially those whose questions indicate that they have not been listening. **Contempt** is sometimes shown to leaders who are especially inept. **Surprise** is another rarity. Although parties may be surprised that a member said or did something, there is usually an attempt to "cover it up."

Monitoring should include looking for these emotions on the faces of others, but it should also include paying close attention to what kinds of signals you are transmitting. Close monitoring will help you know who is having eye contact with the boss. Who is bored? What is agreeing with the speaker? Who is indicating disagreement? As a leader and as a member it is important to ask those who appear to be in disagreement whether they are, in fact, disagreeing. If a member has her arms crossed, what does that mean? It may mean contempt, but it may mean that the temperature in the room is too cold. Who is taking notes? Who seems well-prepared for the meeting? Who seems to be poorly prepared?

Physical Appearance

Most members of professional groups dress in a similar fashion. Males tend to wear navy or gray suits, with white shirts, and blue or red ties. Women tend to wear navy or gray skirted suits and white, blue, yellow, or pink blouses. Of course, in today's world of dot-com companies, some of this has changed. Nevertheless the "professional uniform" remains in most of the corporate world. Individuals should wear little jewelry. For the woman, earrings, a watch, and a wedding ring would be most common. For men, a wedding ring and a watch are usually sufficient. Jewelry indicative of a religious or political group should be avoided (Molloy, 1988; Molloy, 1996). Informal dress may be worn on "casual days." However, casual does not mean extremely casual. Perhaps a man would wear a tie without the coat. Women, too, might eliminate the coat of such days. Dressing for work, though, means just that. One should not dress for anything else at work and expect to be respected.

Haptics
Touching in business is usually held to the shaking of hands. If the other members appear to do this at a meeting, you should do so also. Any other touching, including self touch should be avoided in meetings. The most common types of haptic behavior in group problem-solving situations is the handshake. Do the interactants shake hands before the meeting? Do they shake hands after the meetings? To some extent, a handshake at the end of a meeting is a positive in that nonverbally the interactants are agreeing to the outcome. In many ways, it is similar to a bargain. When the members shake hands, they have "agreed" to the outcomes of the meeting.

Vocalics
Vocalics is the study of how we use the voice. Generally, those with the louder voices will be taken more seriously. A loud, articulate voice provides the speaker with a certain amount of dynamism resulting in higher credibility. In many cases, some group members are unduly influenced by these more dynamic speakers who may deliver a stronger message in terms of intensity but whose comments may lack the content needed to resolve the problems that the group is encountering.

Special attention should be paid to group members who appear to be less involved, who are more apprehensive. These members may have much to offer the group, but they may be intimidated by the loud voices in the group. Each member should take it upon herself to bring the shy members into the decision making. Many times, these shy members have been listening more carefully than some others. If nothing else, these members might be able to contribute by summarizing what has been said.

In today's world, we should also take note of intercultural differences. Many of the members of the group may not be native English speakers. Group members need to listen carefully and analyze what is being said. In terms of content, these members provide additional sources of information from the viewpoint of another culture. Sometimes these members may be misunderstood. It is important that members ask them to repeat or to provide their information in some other way.

Proxemics

Where individuals sit in a group meeting provides a great deal of information about what is likely to happen. We know, for example, that those sitting across from one another are more likely to be argumentative with one another. People who sit away from the table are less likely to get involved in the group deliberations. Those who sit across from the group leader are more likely to participate simply because they have eye contact with the leader.

People who sit next to one another probably like one another, unless there is some pre-established seating mechanism. The concept of liking one another is based on the following theory of interpersonal attraction. For the most part, people choose to be around others who are more similar to themselves. In the case of a group meeting, it may well be that the individuals are seated next to each other because they like each other, and they like each other because they have similar views on the topic. The problem with this from the perspective of the group as a whole is that the members may be seated in cliques. When cliques are seated together, the group may form a confrontational environment.

Developing a Perspective

There can be little doubt that we are incapable of ascertaining what is going on the mind of another person in the group. Certainly any attempt at doing so in the beginning is an impossibility. However, as we get to know how the group functions, we become more knowledgeable about how the group functions and what the various members are thinking as we go through the meetings. Here we will discuss how the process of perspective building works within the group.

Beginning Phase

As a new member of the group or at the beginnings of a new group, it is important to withhold judgments and inferences about what is going on in the meetings. One way of doing this is to maintain an analysis of the amount of participation in the group. That is, who is talking? How much is she/he talking? While you may not want to make a chart while attending a meeting, there may be a way of taking some notes in such a way to indicate later to yourself what is going on in the meeting. Smith (1965) suggests the Flow of Contributions chart to show this (see Figure 6.1).

Flow of Contributions

The Flow of Contributions chart provides an idea of how many times during a meeting a particular member talked. It does not tell us who addressed whom. It tells us little about the quality of what is being said. It also tells us little about the relevance of what has been said. A comment such as, "Could you pass the sugar?" is given equal weight with, "I think we need to move on to the implementation stage," or "Jim, you really haven't commented on this." However, taking note of the number of comments is a good beginning point. If we can establish a chart of where people sit in an earlier meeting, we can determine what effects are there when one of the members of absent from the meeting. The Flow of Contributions can also be affected by people changing seats or by one member's being tardy for the meeting.

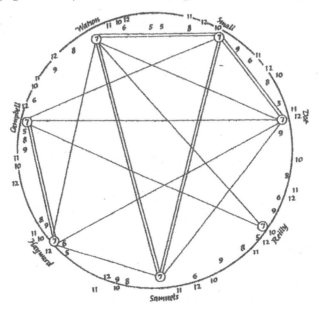

Figure 6.1 Flow of Contributions Chart

Pattern Phase

In Smith's (1965) Pattern of Contributions we can a better idea of how the group is functioning. Because the arrows are pointed in a certain direction, we can tell not only who is talking how much but also we can tell to whom the comment is directed. As noted in Figure 6.2, we can also tell the length of the comments. While this chart still does not tell us anything about the value of the contribution, it does tell us who is taking up the time of the group. Dominating the time of the group can be especially damaging to the group if the dominator is talking so much for the "wrong reasons." However, we will discuss this later in this chapter. With the Pattern of Contributions we know who talked, how much they talked, and to whom the comments were directed.

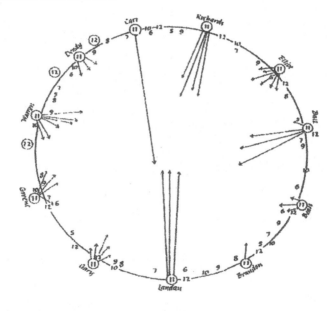

Figure 6.2 Patterns of Contributions

Targeting Phase

In the Targeting (On and Off the Pattern) we find that Smith (1965) has provided us an even better mechanism for assessing group work. In the targeting phase, the observer can tell not only who is talking with whom but also whether the substance of the content is on target. That is, is the comment relevant for this particular time? Is this

something that the group needs to know to move on with the decision-making process at this time? There can be little question that
there are often comments made for purposes other than strictly
moving the discussion forward; sometimes they are relevant and
sometimes they are not (see Figure 6.3).

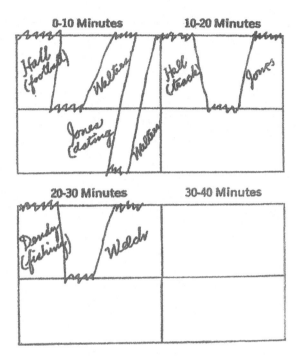

Figure 6.3 Targeting Phase

Verbal Communication

In the targeting phase, we have discussed whether comments are on
target and whether they are relevant to the talk at hand. We will now
discuss several possible types of comments that one may make in a
group meeting to evaluate them for relevance and significance. A
comment may be relevant but not significant. A comment may be
significant but not relevant. Obviously, the best comments are those
that are both relevant and significant. We will add a third type of
comment, one that we will refer to as a ***process comment***, a comment which allows the group to move forward although, at the time,
it may not sound especially significant or relevant.

Lack of Communication

When most of us were in graduate school, we received a version of the story below which illustrates the problem with assumptions, even when only two people are talking with one another. One of our graduate professors provided this story to us.

> The year is 1955, and the British Government's policy of socialized medicine has been extended to include "proxy Papas." That is, any married women not having a child in the first five years of marriage must receive the services of a Government man, who will attempt to be the means of her becoming a mother. The purpose is to repopulate Great Britain after the large number of deaths from World War II. The Smiths have no family, and the Government man is due. Mr. Smith leaves for work. He has a hang dog look as he dutifully pecks his wife at the door.

> MR. SMITH: I'm off. The Government man should be here early.

> He leaves and his wife pretties herself, putting on her most seductive negligee. But instead of the Government man, a door-to-door photographer, specializing in baby pictures, knocks on the door.

> MRS. SMITH: Oh, good morning.

> MAN: You probably don't know me, but I represent . . .

> MRS. SMITH: Oh yes, you needn't explain. My husband said to expect you.

> MAN: I make a specialty of babies, especially twins.

> MRS. SMITH: That's what my husband said. Please sit down.

> MAN: Then your husband probably told you that . . .

> MRS. SMITH: Oh, yes. We both agreed it's the thing to do.

MAN: Well, in that case, we might as well get started.

MRS. SMITH (BLUSHING): Well, where do we start?

MAN: Just leave everything to me, madam. I recommend two in the bathtub, one on the couch and a couple on the floor.

MRS. SMITH: Bathtub, floor. No wonder Harry and I...

MAN: Well, dear lady, even the best of us can't guarantee a good one every time. But say, one of six, one is bound to be a honey. I usually have the best luck with shots in the bathtub.

MRS. SMITH: Pardon me, but it does seem a bit informal . . .

MAN: No, indeed. In my line, a man can't do his best work in a hurry. (HE OPENS HIS ALBUM AND SHOWS THE BABY PICTURES TO HER). Look at this baby. It's a job, took four hours, but isn't she a beauty?

MRS. SMITH. Yes, a lovely child.

MAN: But a tough assignment. Look at this baby. Believe it or not, it was done on top of a bus in Piccadilly Circus.

MRS. SMITH: My God!

MAN: It's not hard when a man knows his job. My work is a pleasure. I spent long years perfecting my technique. Now like this baby—I did it with one shot in Alexandre's window.

MRS. SMITH: I can't believe it.

MAN: And here's a picture of the prettiest twins in town. They turned out exceptionally well when you consider that their mother was so—so difficult. But I knocked off the job in Hyde Park on a snowy afternoon. It took from two in the afternoon until five in the evening. I never worked under such difficulty. People were crowded all around, four or five deep, pushing to get a look.

MRS. SMITH: Four or five deep?

MAN: Yes. And more than three hours. But I had two bobbies helping me. I could have done another shot before dark, but by that time the squirrels were nibbling at my equipment and I had to give up. Well, madam, if you're ready, I'll set up my tripod and get to work.

MRS. SMITH: *Tripod?*

MAN: Yes. I always use a tripod to rest my equipment on. It's much too heavy for me to hold for any length of time. Mrs. Smith! Good Lord! Mrs. Smith, have you fainted?

While the above story is not true (it was, in fact, a contrivance of some graduate students), it does describe in a humorous way how the concept of communication may be believed by all but is used by none. The problem, of course, is that while the parties were using the same language, they were operating from a different set of assumptions. Not only that, but they maintained their own assumptions and believed the other was in agreement the entire time. This shows us how important it is to make certain that we are operating on the same page. The first principle of language, then, is that it should be **clear.** Had Mrs. Smith not interrupted the man during their initial exchange, she would have discovered that he represented a photography company, and the problem would have been abated.

Accuracy and Appropriateness

Language should also be **accurate.** In meetings, one man should listen carefully to whether the words accurately portray what the participants mean. For example, the words "persuade," "entice," "humiliate," and "seduce" may all deal with some form of persuasion; yet some are more negative than others. Some are also more powerful than others. In monitoring the talk during meetings, we need to carefully evaluate how accurate the participants are being.

How powerful their words may be will also affect the remainder of the proceedings.

Appropriate language is also a key in understanding the meeting. Cursing and the like have no place in meetings, but some members tend to use such vocabularies anyway. In some ways, these individuals appear to believe that these words give them more power. Often, however, this inappropriate language will have what is called a "boomerang effect," in that it will lessen the power of those who use it.

Waffling and Bullying

From what we have said about language, it is obvious that language is a powerful tool in group meetings. While *waffling* and *bullying* may sound like opposite processes, in many ways they are similar. When one is waffling, not "showing her cards," this means that the individual is holding on to her power. She usually will not state her goals in a forthright manner. She is saving the information so that she can use it later. Bullying is much more short term. The individual who uses bullying is trying to get his way right away. He is impatient. Both, however, are means of utilizing power in the group situation. In Table 7.4 (below), we show a checklist for observing language in the meeting.

Table 7.4 Observing Language

Person	Accurate	Po	Bu
A.			
B.			
C.			
D.			
E.			
F.			
G.			

Interrupting

One final aspect of monitoring and observing is interruptions. *Interruptions* may or may not be used as power devices in meetings. Both men and women interrupt others, but there are different types of interruptions, and the gender is often the key to the type of interruption that is used. Men more often use the interruption to get the talker to yield the floor. This is referred to by Tannen (1994) as a **negative interruption,** in the sense that it stops someone else from speaking. It is not only a tool of men, however. It is often used when one is excited and impatient. A **positive interruption** is when a comment by the talker has triggered the interrupter to a thought, which complements what the talker is saying. For example, the interrupter might say: "I agree with that, and I would like to add . . . ." Women use positive interruptions more often than do men. A **neutral interruption** in a two-person conversation might be: "Could we get some more coffee?" While it is used by both men and women, it stops the point of the conversation.

Summary

The use of verbal and nonverbal language helps us determine what is going on with the members of the group. When we monitor, we should be careful to observe more so than evaluate or judge. The purpose of observing is to better understand what is happening in the group. In this monitoring, we look for kinesic behavior or gestures as well as touching, physical appearance, and vocalics. In addition, we observe the language taking place to see if it is clear, appropriate, and accurate. Finally, we listen for interruptions to determine their type. The emphasis is whether the group is on topic and whether progress is going to be made in making a decision that is fruitful to all members of the group.

References

Molloy, J. T. (1988). *The new dress for success book.* New York: Warner.

Molloy, J. T. (1996). *New women's dress for success.* New York: Warner

Smith, W. S. (1965). *Group problem-solving through discussion: A process essential to democracy.* Indianapolis: Bobbs-Merrill.

Tannen, D. (1994). *Gender and discourse.* New York: Oxford University Press.

CHAPTER 8

IMPLEMENTATION

Roger left the meeting with a grin on his face. Unlike many groups in which he had participated, he left this meeting with a sense of pride in a job well done. The group had put aside their personal biases and developed a solid and workable plan for improving the productivity of the company's sagging distribution center. It was, he thought, meetings like this that make the process worthwhile.

Over the next few weeks, though, his sense of elation gradually faded. Two group members—Joe and Bob—retired, and their portions of the follow-up work had not been completed. Meanwhile, Edward, the head of the distribution center was fighting some of the changes, convinced that the new procedures were a criticism of his past performance and a subversive means of undermining his power.

The plan, it seemed, was flawless. But the implementation of the plan was full of flaws: a group decision that can't be implemented is a relatively worthless product. Indeed, as Hybels & Weaver (1986) noted, "The test of a group's success is whether it can come up with ideas and a course of action that can be implemented" (p. 226). Given that obvious situation, what could have been done differently to increase the success of the new program? Past research has identified several factors that contribute to implementation success. The most common of these are: (1) participant involvement, (2) management of details, (3) delegation of authority, (4) accountability, and (5) evaluation of the plan.

Factors Contributing to Successful Implementation

Participant Involvement

One secret to successful implementation starts before the group even has its first meeting—with the selection of the members of the group. Ideally, anyone who is essential to the successful implementation of the decision should be involved in that decision. In Roger's case, the decision not to have the head of the distribution center involved in the group was a fatal flaw. Without that person's cooperation, the chances of successful implementation were minimal.

A key player such as Edward is not the only one whose participation becomes important, though. If the plan is to work, all group members must be supportive. Any group member who leaves the discussion believing that the wrong decision has been made will be detrimental to the group effort, particularly if they feel that their input was ignored. If their views have been dismissed by the group, their participation in the group becomes a liability. Take the case of Joe and Bob, two members who retired before the plan was put into effect. They could have undermined the project in two different manners. Joe didn't like the solution chosen by the group from the beginning. Most other members liked the idea, though, and he and Bob were ultimately out-voted. Resentful, Joe simply used the organization's informal grapevine to voice his displeasure. Soon rumors were circulating that the new idea wouldn't work for a variety of reasons. By the time the upper administration realized what was happening, Joe had retired and was no longer with the company.

Bob, meanwhile, realized that his department would be playing a key role in the implementation process. He simply created a series of barriers within his division that slowed the entire process, grinding parts of it to a halt. When others complained, he noted that he would be retiring soon and somebody else would need to take over his role anyway. By the time he retired, and with the other problems faced by the project, it died a slow death within the organization.

How do you counter such problems? Start before the decision is made. Consider what could have happened, though, if Edward had been part of the group discussion from the beginning. He would have followed the group process from the onset, heard and participated in a discussion of all of the problems and barriers faced by his division. He could have provided them with first-hand information on the source of many of the problems. By the time the group reached the decision-making stage, he would have contributed his own ideas for solving the problem to the group. Some of his suggestions would likely be incorporated into the final decision, and he would understand the group's reasons for not including others. When the decision is ultimately made, he would understand why each element was necessary for the full implementation of this new plan. He would be someone who would contribute to making the plan work, not a barrier to a workable idea.

What about Joe and Bob? They were members of the group, but still emerged as barriers to implementation. The key in their cases is a factor known as *process disruption*. If the discussion process is disrupted or faulty, then the quality of the decision will be inferior and more difficult to implement (Leathers, 1969). Joe and Bob's problem was that their viewpoints were never fully considered by the group. Once the group realized it had a workable solution, it rushed through the final stages of the discussion. That shortened the meeting time, but left Joe and Bob unable to express their views. Even if the group ultimately discards their suggestions, they must leave the group with the feeling that their views were at least considered.

The key to doing this is by recognizing the need to do so at an early point in the discussion. At some point, well before the meeting is over, you start to recognize what the decision is going to be. Fisher (1970) called this phenomenon *decision emergence*. At that point, the focus of further discussion should be on gaining support from all group members for implementation. This process is known as *consensus building*. The communication necessary for consensus building requires active participation on the parts of each member. This not only produces a decision that is acceptable to the group members, but one that they are also more enthusiastic about. The goal here is member satisfaction. Member satisfaction contributes to three distinct factors: (1) enjoyment of the group process, (2) a better quality of output, and (3) pride in group membership (Cragan, 1991, p. 21). If all group members enjoy the group process and feel pride in group membership, they will produce a better decision and work to see it implemented.

Management of Details

A plan works when the details work. Implementation requires more than a simple decision to do something. The decision should also involve specific assignment of tasks, with specific individuals responsible for handling the details of each task. For most major group decisions, no single person has the time or capability to ensure implementation of the plan. The entire group shares that responsibility. As Hybels and Weaver (1986) noted, "A good leader should be able to delegate responsibility to the group members" p. 239). The secrets here are three-fold: (1) a willingness to delegate authority to others, (2) providing those people with the tools that they need to be successful, and (3) verifying that they are progressing on their assignments. If the group fails in any of these aspects, the project will probably not succeed.

First, consider the following example. During the Normandy Invasion of World War II, allied troops were given specific targets that each unit was supposed to hit. When the units got ashore, however, many discovered that their targets had been deserted. No problem. The commanders of each unit, working with delegated authority, simple chose alternative targets and went after those. At the same time, German commanders found themselves facing an enemy that had attacked in an unexpected manner and in an unexpected place, but none of the German commanders had the delegated authority to order a shift in battle plans for their units. By the time approval for new orders had been received from German high command, the American and British forces had an unbreakable foothold on the beaches of Normandy. While most group decisions won't be that dramatic, the principle is the same. Somebody has to be given the responsibility of achieving a particular goal, and they must have the authority to see that the goal is implemented. The concept here should be *equifinality*. The group may be unable to anticipate all of the details that must be addressed before a particular aspect of the decision can be implemented. Still, someone should be working on that aspect with the final goal in mind, making adjustments to the plan as progress is made. The effective group leader works with a similar willingness to delegate authority.

Second, the group must provide the delegated worker with the resources to get the job done. Cragan and Wright (1991) noted that the group leader has a responsibility to provide a delegated worker with the materials, tools and information needed to accomplish the task. Zeuschner (1993) noted the resources are often crucial to successful implementation. "If resources and rewards are plentiful, it is fairly easy to get different small groups within an organization to cooperate. However, as is more often the case, if resources are limited, there will be a competitive atmosphere in the organization.... At its worst, it can lead to the deliberate sending of misinformation, secrecy, suspicion, and even sabotage." (p. 205). In fact, little is accomplished if you ask someone to get a celebrity speaker for your next banquet, but provide them with no budget to pay for the speaker's fee, their travel expenses, or their hotel room. Quite the contrary, the worker who is assigned such a task will become frustrated at their inability to carry out the assignment; their growing resentment against the organization will become a barrier that will interfere with successful implementation of that and other projects. If the group lacks the resources to achieve a particular aspect of a project, then it should simply reassess its goals and work toward something which can be achieved without creating frustration on the part of its members.

Finally, successful implementation requires that the group carefully monitor the work of each of its members. Some system of progress reports must be established so that those members how have delegated assignments can provide updates on the progress that they are making. The intervals on these progress reports should be spaced in such a manner that adjustments can be made for those who don't make as much progress as was expected. That's an inevitable consequence of the group process. The group as a whole will tend to underestimate the time that it will take to accomplish some particular goal of the group. If there is no buffer zone in the implementation plan, allowing time to adjust for such miscalculations, it may be difficult to complete the project (at least, to complete it on time).

Accountability
Schultz (1989) noted that "Accountability is an inherent component of the implementation process" (p. 166). The key to accountability, she added, was to ensure that each member have a clear understanding of what was expected of them. She suggested a list of six questions that could be used to increase accountability (pp. 166-167). They are:

1. "What is our task and how shall we do it?"
2. "Who will be responsible for carrying out the proposed plan?"
3. "When can our group reasonably expect results?"
4. "What unplanned events or accidents are likely to jeopardize our plans?"
5. "What people should we consult who can help us with our proposal?"
6. "What people could threaten our proposal?"

The general purpose of such questions are twofold. First, they ensure that the group will not assume that its job is done simply because they made a decision. Instead, the group understands that its job is not done until the solution has been implemented. Second, it provides a means of ensuring that each member understands what is expected of them, a condition that increases the chances of successful implementation (Patton & Giffin, 1978, 170-178).

Evaluation and Adjustment

Don't be afraid to admit you're wrong. As Hybels and Weaver (1986) noted, "Sometimes groups come up with plans that don't work" (p. 226). In fact, the reason that some decisions are never implemented is simply that they're bad decisions that won't work. When that happens, the group must be willing to re-evaluate and make adjustments.

Evaluation must be an on-going process, one that should continue all during the group process. Further, it's extremely important that the evaluation process continue after the decision is made. Some organizations may institutionalize this process, with built-in procedures for looking at a solution after it has been in effect for a while.

That sounds relatively easy. In practice, it can be difficult. Some organizational members may have personal or organizational interests that interfere with an accurate evaluation process. After the U.S. government authorized testing and development of the Osprey aircraft, for example, an evaluation process was built into the contract. However, some members of the military who supported the project subsequently falsified some maintenance records to show a better performance evaluation for the aircraft. Failure to fairly and effectively evaluate that decision led to the deaths of several military personnel when one of the aircraft crashed during a training exercise. Not all evaluation processes have such vital outcomes, but the example does illustrate the need for evaluation. It's better to admit that you and the group made a mistake at an early stage in the evaluation process than to stubbornly persist on sticking with a solution that will not work.

Working within the Organization

Even if Roger's group had done everything right, and come up with a workable solution, there's still a chance that it would not have been implemented. The problem: Roger's division within the organization may not have the power to implement all elements of the plan. Within any organization, in fact, there are many groups which have to be considered in the implementation of any plan. The factors involved in working on inter-group factors can be just as complicated, or even more so, than any individual group process. As Zeuschner (1993) noted, "Many of the characteristics of small groups—networks and patterns, personal influences, leadership, and outcomes—are also seen in the larger, multiple groups system of the organization" (p. 204). To get a plan implemented, one group often needs the help of another group or groups. Meanwhile, the plan is likely to face opposition or competition from another group within the same organization. Most organizational members (particularly managers and administrators) are members of at least two groups within the organizations, and their roles in those groups are often at conflict with each other.

The competitive nature of inter-organizational groups seems to be something that's impossible to avoid. All groups within the organization typically compete with each other for a limited amount of scarce resources which are allocated by higher administrators or executives. As a result, organizational groups may become more competitive toward each other than they will toward an outside competitor who is their major rival.

One of the barriers your project will face will be *secrecy*, i.e., a lack of available information from other groups within the organization. Inter-organizational groups routinely withhold information from each other. Thus Cragan and Wright (1991) noted "each group does not communicate all of its information to the rest of the organization, nor does the organization communicate all of its information upward" (p. 259). This tendency to withhold information increases as groups become more competitive. Similarly, insecurity on the part of a group supervisor can increase the tendency toward secrecy. Informal communication channels, the infamous grapevine, are often developed to supplement the process as each group seeks to acquire the "secret" information from others (Cragan & Wright, 1991, p. 260).

In these instances, the grapevine often develops through two sources. First, some members of your group will also share membership in other groups within the organization. Middle management workers are members of at least two groups, the one in which they are the leader and an administrative subgroup in which they participate as a lower level employee. Other workers may have a primary work group while working on an organizational-wide committee with other people. Some grapevine networks are developed outside the workplace, as organizational members participate in social activities with each other. Over time, these multiple contacts become a means of transmitting "secret" information to members of your group.

Another intergroup factor which can inhibit implementation is *deadline substitution*. Many organizations work on precise and important deadlines for the production of their work product. Further, the process is often serial in nature, with the completion of one step in the process necessary before the next group can begin its work on the project. As Cragan and Wright (1991) noted, "In this environment each work group wants the maximum amount of time to do its step in the manufacturing process. The situation sets up the classic case of deadline substitution so that the grapevine becomes very active as each work group tries to identify the 'real deadlines'" (p. 261).

Regardless of which external group barriers are present, though, implementation success depends upon them recognized and faced. Cooperation (or at least, not opposition) from other groups within the organization significantly eases the implementation process. Building networks outside the group is the long-term answer to this problem.

Situational Factors

Several situational factors can influence the implementation stage. Two of the major situational factors that must be considered are (1) the nature of the group and (2) the history of the group.

Nature of the Group. Implementation is easier with some groups than others. In most organizational groups, the implementation process may be tedious, but there is usually sufficient motivation for each member to do their part. In that instance, implementation depends upon (as noted above) understanding the group's role in the organization and gaining the participation of key organizational members. Implementing a solution is harder when the group is composed of volunteers. Civic organizations, for example, often rely upon volunteers to carry out many of their functions. The advantage of volunteer groups is their low labor costs and a membership structure of people who are committed to the organization's goals. On the negative side, though, a group leader has limited means for offering rewards and punishments to group members. Further, no matter how sincerely a volunteer may support the organization, they still have outside commitments in other facets of their lives which will interfere with implementation. In such instances, it is imperative that the group leader maintain close contact with members. That personal contact becomes a means of providing positive verbal feedback while monitoring progress on the project.

History of the Group. The implementation process is easier if the group members have known each other for some time, have worked together successfully before, and share a common perception of the group's goals. Implementation is difficult if the group members have a history of antagonistic relationships or one in which previous projects have been unsuccessful. In such instances, individual members will not trust others to do their share of the work and can then use that argument for not doing their own work. Some groups have no history at all. Class projects, for example, are often composed groups in which the members have never worked with each other before. When that occurs, some early portion of the implementation process must be spent on identifying skills within the group that can be used to contribute to its implementation.

Implementation Techniques
Some organizations use specific techniques to increase the chances of successful implementation. Two of the most popular are the PERT technique and the use of project teams.

PERT (Program Evaluation and Review Technique)
PERT was developed to help implement solutions which are highly complicated and involved a variety of details. It is particularly useful when the solution involves (1) a variety of necessary materials, (2) several people whose work must be coordinated, and (3) a series of steps that must be completed in a specific sequence (Brilhart, Galanes, & Adams, 2001). PERT provides a means of expediting those details and keeping track of each step in the process. Siebold (1992) identified eight distinct steps that the group should use when following the PERT approach.

1. Describe the final step (how the solution should appear when fully operational).

2. List any events that must occur before the final goal is completed.

3. Place these events into a chronological order

4. If necessary, develop a flow diagram of the process and the steps in the process.

5. List all the activities, resources, and materials needed to accomplish each step.

6. Estimate the time needed to accomplish each step. Total those estimates to get a total time needed for implementing the plan.

7. Compare the total time estimate with deadlines or expectations and make necessary adjustments.

8. Determine which members will be responsible for each step.

The advantage of the PERT approach is that it provides a means of organizing the implementation process, making task assignments in a systematic manner, and providing a checklist that can be used to monitor the process. As a result, group members have a clear understanding of their individual roles in the process, while the group leader has a means for ensuring accountability of each participant.

The Project Team

Sometimes an organization will create a special group for the implementation of a group decision. The resulting *project team* will consist of individuals who have special expertise that can be applied to the project and who will work together to accomplish a common goal (Wood, 1997, pp. 288-289). A project team has a number of implementation advantages. Tasks can be delegated on the basis of the skills of each team member (Cragan & Wright, 1991). Each participant can be selected on the basis of an expertise that can be useful to implementing the task. In this manner, the project team has the advantage of working with people's strengths, not their weaknesses. At the same time, no single group member has to be an expert on all phases of the assignment. They can draw on each others' expertise and coordinate their activities for maximum implementation effect.

As Wood (1997) noted, "A project team is valuable when many individuals will work on a single project, and what each person does has implications for other members of the team" (p. 289). In most cases, though, the standard elements of successful implementation are necessary. Participant involvement is critical. Authority must be delegated so that individual team members are responsible for handling specific details, and the group must constantly be willing to reevaluate the project and to make necessary adjustments.

Summary

A solution that can't be implemented has little value. Once a group has gone to the time and effort to develop a solution to any specific problem, they should also take a little extra time to ensure that it can be implemented.

Several factors can contribute to implementation success. Participant involvement is important; implementation is easier to achieve if the people responsible for putting the plan into effect also had a role in developing that plan. As the implementation stage progresses, the group leader must attend to the management of details. An accountability plan increases the effectiveness of each individual member. The group must constantly evaluate their progress and be willing to make adjustments.

Further, groups are often part of a larger organization, and the nature of that organization must be considered. In that instance, implementation often depends upon the ability of the group (particularly the group leader) to work with other groups within the organization.

Other situational factors which may affect implementation are the nature of the group and the history of the group. Implementation is often more difficult if the group is composed entirely of volunteer members, since the leader has less ability to hold members accountable. Implementation is easier if the group has a history of success on other projects.

Finally, at least two implementation techniques are available to group leaders. PERT (Program Evaluation and Review Technique) is a checklist of eight specific steps which allows the group to keep track of the details necessary for implementation. A project team is a special group of individuals created by an organization for the implementation of a group decision. Project teams are created by bringing together individuals who have special expertise that can be applied to the project and who will work together to accomplish a common goal.

By the use of such techniques, a group can increase the chances that its decision will be implemented.

References

Brilhart, J. K., Galanes, G. J., & Adams, K. (2001). *Effective group discussion: Theory and practice.* Boston: McGraw-Hill.

Cragan, J. F., & Wright, D. W. (1991). *Communication in small group discussions.* St. Paul, MN: West Publishing.

Fisher, B. A. (1970). Decision emergence: Phases in group decision making. *Speech Monographs, 37,* 53-66.

Hybels, S., & Weaver, R. L., (1986). *Communicating effectively.* New York: Random House.

Leathers, D. G. (1969). Process disruption and measurement of small group communication. *Quarterly Journal of Speech, 55,* 287-300.

Patton, B. R., & Griffin, K. (1978). *Decision-making group interaction.* New York: Harper & Row.

Schultz, B. G. (1989). *Communicating in the small group: Theory and practice.* New York: Harper & Row.

Siebold, D. R. (1992). Making meetings more successful: Plans, formats, and procedures for group problem solving. In R. S. Cathcart & L. A. Samovar, *Small group communication: A reader,* 6th ed. (p. 178-191). Dubuque, IA: Wm. C. Brown.

Wood, J. T. (1997). *Communication in our lives.* Belmont, CA: Wadsworth.

Zeuschner, R. (1993). *Communicating today* (2nd ed.). Boston: Allyn & Bacon.

SOMETHING TO THINK ABOUT
VIRTUAL MEETINGS

A quick search on Google will tell you that businesses are becoming more and more interested in the concept of "Virtual meetings". These are meetings held without face-to-face contact and use a variety of technologies that allow both real time (instant messaging) and short time (e-mail) communication.

1. Is this making us more or less productive?

2. Is this giving us more or less free time?

3. What elements of meetings are missing when held "virtually?"

4. Are the various pressures for conformity stronger or weaker in "virtual" meetings?

5. What about people who have a hard time communicating in face-to-face groups, will this help them or make things worse?

CHAPTER 9

LEADERSHIP

Much of what you've read elsewhere in this book will play itself out in this chapter. Leadership is one of the most pivotal variables in successful group communication and performance. For many students it's the reason they study group communication. It may be the reason you went to college in the first place.

When you think of leadership, your mind may conjure images of presidents and social leaders. You may think of teachers, ministers and others who have influenced your life. You may think of friends who have always seem to get their way, people who you have followed in life. In a way, leadership is what leaders do.

One of the more popular definitions of leadership was provided by Shaw, "Leadership is an influence process which is directed towards goal achievement" (1981, p. 31). At first blush it may seem like Shaw is talking about persuasiveness and exercising power. While these functions may fall under the umbrella of leadership, they are not an inclusive list. Think about all that you've learned about groups so far, flip ahead and look at what you will learn. Everything in your class, everything in this book is trying to help you move your groups towards goal achievement. In a very real sense, leadership is that act of being in a group.

In this chapter we will examine leadership from the; **Facilitation, Persuasiveness, Perceived Leadership, Syntality,** and **Functional** perspectives. The issues of leadership style and use of power will also be discussed.

Facilitation

Mention the term leader or leadership in most modern American organizations and the terms **Manager** or **Management** immediately come to mind. If you asked a member of an organization who their leader was, they would likely point to their direct manager, or perhaps a committee chair, or team leader that they work closely with. Hickson and Stacks (1998) argue that, "a good manager is a good leader" (p. 158). However, they may not necessarily be the same thing.

For the most part, management has come to mean controlling the flow of communication. If you look at a typical organizational chart, those black lines that connect the little boxes represent **lines of authority**. More simply, they represent who talks to whom. It is, therefore, the responsibility of managers to control what information gets passed up or down through the organization.

For example, a fairly routine decision that is made in every college every year regards granting tenure and promotion to certain professors. These decisions are usually initiated by an application on the part of the professor who seeks the promotion. This requests, along with extensive supporting materials, is presented to the department Chair who will form a committee within the department to evaluate the application. The committee will vote on the application and report back to the departmental Chair. The Chair will, in turn, report to her Dean. The Dean then hands the decision to a school wide committee who evaluates the materials and reports back to the Dean. Based on this report the Dean makes a decision and hands it to a Provost or Vise President. This person makes a decision and hands it to the University President. The University President may have to get approval from a board of Trustees before granting the promotion.

To be sure, each of these people and groups acts as a gate keeper. A negative decision at any point will likely kill the request. But in the case of approval, where is the decision being made? Where is the leadership? The various committees have no real power, nor in fact do most of the administrators. All they do is hand the decision up the line. By the time the problem gets to the person who has actual authority to make the actual decision, it becomes a rubber stamp. Everyone from below points up saying, "We're just advisory." The people at the top point down saying, "We're just supporting our administrators." *In fact, in most modern American organizations, the buck doesn't stop anywhere.*

It is therefore important to understand just what a manager does. For the most part he or she is a **gatekeeper**. A gatekeeper's main function is to decide what information moves through his or her office. This is no small task in the information age. Shielding subordinates from unneeded data, or noise, is a critical function. Likewise, it is important to know what needs to be passed up the line as well.

The manager also spends a great deal of time delegating responsibilities, procuring resources and generally facilitating the interactions within the units they manage. Whether or not these people actually influence any of the decisions and actions within the units remains to be seen. The possibility is there, but it is not a necessity.

Persuasiveness
Perhaps the most traditional view of leadership equates it with persuasiveness and influence. In other part of this text you have read about cohesiveness, Groupthink and Risky (Polarity) Shift. Conformity and pressures of uniformity are such an integral part of the group process that most theorists argue that a group cannot truly be called a small group if such normative pressures do not exist. In your own mind, it is likely that you equate leadership with the ability to influence a group. Shaw (1981) expressed a consensus opinion when he wrote "that leadership is an influence process which is directed toward goal achievement" (p. 31).

The study of persuasiveness is as old as the study of communication itself. Aristotle dedicated a third of his *Rhetoric* to the concept of *Ethos*. Aristotle argued that men who personified the prevailing cultural ethic were credible people who ought to be listened to. In the case to the ancient Greeks, this ethic was personified by the scholar athlete, a perfection of mind and body.

Indeed, contemporary research bolsters Aristotle's belief. The vast preponderance of research finds a very powerful relationship between the perception of competence and persuadability. Mausner and Bloch (1957), Mulder and Wilkye (1970), and Hollander and Julian (1970) have all documented this relationship in one fashion or another.

There are some interesting consequences here. First, research has found that it was **perceived** competence that related to influence, not actual competence. Hollander and Julian (1970) put test subjects in a group and gave clearly bogus feedback as to the quality of the work. The subjects were more persuaded by group members receiving false praise than those receiving false blame. This was true despite the fact that the subjects had the ability to know the feedback was false. The implication is clear, it is better to look competent than to actually be competent.

This is especially true if the subjects have special competencies. The stories of people attaining success because they possessed some special talent are too numerous to recount. One of your authors claims to know more than one professor who was given tenure, not because they were a good teacher or researcher, but because they could work the department's computers better than anyone else.

Ross and Steinmetz (1977) found that people who receive evidence about a person's competency in one field will assume they are competent in another. They called this **Fundamental Attribution Error**. Ask your professor how many times he or she is approached for advice on questions they have no logical competence in. The assumption is; "you have a Ph.D. in communication you must know something about my problem." Students also feel threatened when professors have opinions different from their own. What the student needs to understand is that outside the area of the professors expertise the professor is just another person with an opinion, not necessarily better or worse than anyone else's. Amsbary (1986) found fundamental attribution error was a significant predictor of leadership. Group members would appoint leaders because they demonstrated competencies completely unrelated to the task at hand.

We don't just do this on a personal or group levels; start taking note of how many so called experts on television really aren't. In fact, they are usually some politician or celebrity who has high name recognition, but no special knowledge or ability on the topic of discussion. Clearly, a powerful way to improve your leadership is to possess and demonstrate competencies that the other members of the group don't have.

Perceived Leadership

Without a doubt, perception is a potent determinate of leadership. Moreover, it may in fact be what leadership is. An impressive amount of evidence has been amassed to show that acknowledged leaders may not be any more persuasive than any of the other group members. Rather, group leaders are **believed** to be more persuasive than the others.

In an early study of leadership, Riecken (1958) attempted to see if perceived leaders were any more persuasive than the others. He gave his groups very difficult tasks and then passed notes that contained uniquely elegant solutions to the problems. He initially predicted that the high credible subjects would more easily gain acceptance to this information than the low credible subjects.

To his surprise, almost all of the information made it into the groups' final answers. In other words, the high credible subjects were no more persuasive then the low credible subjects. What was interesting was that the subjects correctly identified that source of the information when it came from the highly credible subjects, but misidentified the source when it came from the low credible subjects. In both cases, they thought the uniquely elegant solutions came from the highly credible subjects.

How many times have you had one of your great ideas stolen by someone who the group already liked? According to Bunyi (1985) this is a very common occurrence. He calls it the **Unsung Hero Phenomenon**. You may be very valuable to the group, but the group, itself, may not recognize this fact. It is possible that you exercise more actual influence than you know, the trick is to be less concerned with the credit and more concerned with the productivity.

The key to this may surprise you. More than anything your value in the group will be determined by how much you talk. The underlying logic to this is that talkativeness shows interest. It does show motivation. This underscores the importance of attending meetings and participating in them. The more you participate, the more highly the group will regard you. Burgoon (1978) found that too much extroversion could diminish your credibility. You must therefore not get carried away.

Syntality

A fourth way to look at leadership has more to do with the "feel" of the group. Remember back to chapter one. A group, by definition, has norms that the members follow. Small groups develop a broad range of normative behaviors that may include the use of time, dress, seating arrangement, appropriate and inappropriate evidence, etc. Cattell (1951) defined this group character or personality as **Syntality**.

In a sense, syntality is a broader form of influence. Rather than focus narrowly on decision-making, it broadens the notion of influence onto the entire group dynamic. Though there is little research that attempts to document leadership emergence and influence in this area, philosophically it remains a sound dimension of concern.

147

From your own experience, note what norms your groups have established. Reflect about the origins of those norms. Would you say that your leader or leaders are largely responsible for these norms?

Functional

In terms of group performance and dynamics the Behavioral approach to leadership is the most useful. The Functional Approach asks the question slightly differently, instead of focusing on leaders and their actions it focuses on groups and on which behaviors move and influence the group. In a sense, the other perspectives are perspectives on leaders and the Functional Approach is a perspective on leadership.

Recall that groups have a task and social dimension. To this end there are behaviors that a productive group needs. The group needs its members to engage in certain task behaviors. To have a productive discussion it needs members to provide data and opinions, to react and be critical, and to elaborate on those ideas.

The group also has a social dimension. Someone has to establish norms, gate keep, be supportive and encouraging, and relieve tensions that develop. Some have called this a Maintenance function.

As you read some of these examples you may think to yourself that the Functional Approach incorporates elements of the other approaches. You were right to think so. One of the advantages of this approach is that it is very broad based. Since it focuses on the group and its needs rather than the leader and his or her characteristics it tends to be more inclusive. In fact a group has many needs.

You also might think that it is nearly impossible for anyone to cover both areas completely. You are right again. Since we are not looking at leaders here, we can redefine leadership as a shared, not a singularly held characteristic. In a sense, everyone in the group is a leader because everyone helps the group move towards its final objective. In this way, concepts like the Unsung Hero Phenomenon are less troubling. If we are less concerned with credit and more concerned with group needs, we are likely to increase productivity.

There are many real world examples of this application. It might surprise you to know that many aspects of the military are structured around this perspective. Even though the military has very formal and rigid channels and rules of authority, the task at hand will often take precedence over them.

In World War II, The United States developed long range high altitude bombers. These were a tremendous departure from the low-level dive-bombers that had heretofore been used. Unlike the earlier weapon systems that only needed one pilot to fly the plane and drop the bombs, these large planes required a pilot, a co pilot and a bombardier. The pilot's job was to get the plane to and from the target, and was in charge during these stages of the mission. When the plane lined up for its bombing run, however, the bombardier was in control and gave orders to the rest of the flight crew, including the pilots.

Modern day S.E.A.L. teams, Ranger units, and Special Forces all follow the same philosophy. Everyone has a role to play and when a particular role is the most important, that member is in charge and everyone follows orders. A student who had been in the Navy once gave a report that talked about on his submarine duty. There were times when everyone, including the Captain, listened to and obeyed the instructions of the Sonar operator who was an enlisted man. It wasn't the rank that was important, it was the job.

Steven Ambrose (1994) noted in study of the D-Day invasion that both the Allied and Axis powers suffered from poor planning. The Germans did not correctly predict where and how the Allies would attack the French coast and the Allied troops often landed on the wrong beaches and had little or no supporting cover. Ambrose argues that it was the Allies adaptability to this chaos that made the difference and helped them carry the day. The German troops were not taught to think and react without command orders, so they waited for orders to redeploy their troops. Meanwhile the Allied troops on the beach made snap decisions and adapted themselves to the situation they found themselves in. So while the German's waited, the Allies acted. Eventually this made all the difference.

In his book *Thriving on Chaos* (1987) Thomas Peters claims that it is an organization's ability to adapt to chaos that will make them successful. So like the soldiers storming the beaches of France, the modern American businessman or woman must be adaptable and must learn to share authority.

Another interesting aspect of the Functional Approach is that almost anyone can find some way to be a leader. Reflect back on your participation in groups. Are you a research hound and have lots of data at your fingertips? Are you the kind of person that doesn't bring much but you spin off the ideas of others and make them better? Both of these things help the group.

The Functional Approach also acknowledges that negative behaviors will develop. As you can see, this approach does not focus on the individual and is not very concerned with taking or hogging credit. Those are, in fact, self-centered functions. These include**; Blocking**, shooting down everyone's ideas; **Dominating**, interrupting and speaking most of the time; **Aggressing**, being verbally hostile to the other group members; **Playing**, distracting the group from its work; **Status Seeking**, taking credit for everything; and **Withdrawing**, avoiding interactions by physically or emotionally removing yourself from the group. All of these behaviors are an attempt to satisfy personal needs at the expense of the group. Like the other categories, it's easy to find yourself on the list of self-centered functions. It then becomes a challenge to work on these behaviors. Some of us need to talk more, some of us need to talk less.

Styles of Leadership

A commonly held belief is that there are two styles of leadership: The Task leader and the Social leader. This is an understandable dichotomy because it reflects the two basic functions of leadership discussed above. The task leader is highly concerned with getting a job done, making sure everyone has a job, that all the bases are covered. The social leader, on the other hand, is concerned with opinions and feelings, wants to make sure the subordinates are happy, and wants to build consensus wherever possible.

Over time the terms have evolved into **Autocratic Leadership** and **Democratic Leadership**. We've also thrown in a third type of leadership that's called **Laissez-Faire**. This leader is not very concerned with either the task or social dimensions. Initially, there was a of research generated to determine which style of leadership was superior. Though most of the studies agreed that the laissez-faire style was not a very productive approach, the data on autocratic and democratic style was not so clear. In some cases the democratic leaders out-performed the autocratic leaders and at other times the converse was true.

There are two major flaws with this dichotomous thinking that help explain why no clear research consensus could emerge. The first is that it is a false dichotomy. The initial model looked something like this:

Task (Autocratic).........................Social (Democratic)

While there is a natural division between autocratic and democratic leadership styles, there is no logical division between the task and social dimensions.

Blake, et al. (1987) posited that concern of task and concern for people were the two major variables of concern regarding leadership but that they were not mutually exclusive concerns. It was possible, and in most cases desireable, to have very high concerns on both dimensions.

They developed their model of leadership in a grid which is one of the most influential models of leadership today (See Figure 8.1). The grid initially identifed five leadership positions.

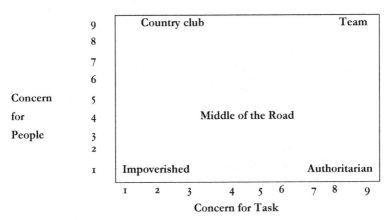

Figure 8.1 Managerial Grid

9,1 Authority-Compliance. This leader has a high concern for task but low concern for the social dimensions of the group. This leader is most closely resembles the traditional autocratic leader. Group members are not expected to participate in decisions and this leader only asks questions to get specific data. This leader wants to get the job done quickly and efficiently and doesn't really care on way or the other how other goup members feel about it.

1,9 Country Club. This leader is highly concerned about the feeling and relationships of the group members. The underlying philosophy is that happy group members will find their own way. Blake et. al. argue that this is not true democratic leadership as many may believe.

1,1 Impoverished. Not concerned with the job or the people, the inpoverished leader most closely resembles the laissez-faire leader.

5,5 Middle of the Road. This leader is not highly concerned with either dimension, rather on striking a balance between the two. It is often frustrating to work with these leaders because you're never sure which concern will win out in a given situation. These leaders often find themselves saying, "Hey I've been too nice and nothings getting done, it's time to crack the whip!" or "I know I've been tough on you guys, what can I do to make you feel better?" Ultimately this leader still believes the productivity comes at the sacrifice of feelings.

9,9 Team Management. This leader is highly concerned with productivity and makes sure the group is on track. The team leader also knows that the social dimensions are important and constantly tries to involve group members in all aspects of the process. Blake et. al. argue that this is true democratic leadership.

Blake et. al. obviously favor the team approach. In most cases they are justified in this bias. Their grid has been widely adopted and adapted throughout the business world. Many companies spend a great deal of time and money teaching their group leaders how to achieve the team perspective.

But is the team approach always the best? The answer is a resounding "No!" Gastil (1994) points out that no one approach is effective in all situations. This leads to the second flaw in the democratic versus autocratic argument, and may explain the early ambiguity of results concerning this conflict.

Fiedler (1967) was one of the first theorists to point out that it's the situation that determines the leader's effectiveness. The situational variables that Fielder identified were; the interpersonal relationships between the leader and the group, position power between the leader and the group, and task complexity. In a nutshell, Fielder found that when the above conditions were extreme, autocratic leaders tended to fair the best, and when the variables were moderate, the democratic leaders fared the best.

It is arguable that the most common case is for the condition to be moderate so the democratic approach is going to be the recommended style. The leader must recognize that when conditions get extreme, a more autocratic approach may be called for.

Leadership and Power

Returning to the issue of influence, it is useful to understand the nature of power when acting as group member. While the terms leadership and power are not interchangeable they certainly are related. The issue of power also blurs the line between **Persuasion** and **Coercion**. When we persuade, we leave the decision up to the target of our persuasion. An add campaign may be very effective and manipulative, but it's still up to us whether we spend our money or not.

Suppose you were asked out on a date by one of your classmates. You might initially feel reluctant, but they may convince you by offering to take you to an expensive restaurant or popular club. This would be persuasion. Now suppose it was your professor who asked you out. Is it the same thing? Probably not. Your professor has the power to evaluate your performance in class. Your professor will assign you a grade that will impact your overall G.P.A. You might fear that the professor will retaliate if you say "no" by hurting your G.P.A. The power in this relationship creates an undeniable element of coercion. Which is why most universities have strict codes of conduct governing such behavior.

Bennis and Nanus (1985) provide us with a very useful list of the sources of power:

1. **Coercive power.** This is basically the power to punish, the classic "do what I want or else!" threat. Many people have coercive power over us. Coercive power can be devastatingly effective, but it can also have some unwanted side effects. First of all the threat has to be perceived and believed. We all know of parents who make threats they never follow through on and the terrors they raise as children. Bosses who constantly threaten to fire employees, but never do, are the company joke. If the subject does not believe you will follow through on your threat, then you don't have the power to change their behavior.

The other problem with coercive power is that it is limited. There are only so many things a boss can do to make your life unpleasant. And of course once it's been done, it can't be done again. A boss can make an employee work weekends as a punishment, but what then? People adapt and get used to unpleasant situations. The boss now needs to find some other way to threaten the employee. We've all know parents who spank their children many times a day. It seems like these kids are impervious to the punishment and just consider it part of life. They also tend to be unruly children.

The last problem with coercive power is that it causes resentment on the subject. People (especially Americans) have a natural resentment when their options are limited by someone else. They may comply, but their commitment to that compliance is limited. If you have the ability to coerce your group members and then exercise that power, don't expect that they'll work very hard towards the group's objectives. Also, don't be surprised if they find subtle ways to undermine you.

2. Reward Power. Some people see reward power as the opposite of coercive power, others see it as the other side of the same coin. Implicit in a person's ability to offer rewards for compliance is their ability to not reward. If you are denied an expected reward do you perceive that as a punishment?

Psychologically there seems to be a big difference however. Experienced educators find those teachers who give points for attendance are thought to be much nicer than teachers who take points away for absences. If you have to attend ten classes and the teacher says, "You have 100 attendance points and you'll lose ten every time you miss," they are disliked. If, on the other hand, the teacher says, "I'll give you ten points every time you come to class," they are loved. Even though in reality, they are doing the exact same thing. The difference is that the first teacher seems to be taking something away, while the second seems to be giving something.

Regarding compliance, the offer of rewards is usually very effective. But like coercive power, rewards usually have a limit. You can only offer so many bonuses, raises or promotions.

3. Legitimate Power. This is power that comes from a position, not a person. Police officer, judges, clergy, teachers, etc. would all be people with position power. At first blush it may seem like legitimate power is just a formalized way to reward and punish. Certainly rewards and punishments do play a role, but there is a deeper issue.

We generally respect these people not only because they can hurt us, but because of who they are. Juries tend to believe the testimony of police officers over defendants. There's just something about the office. If a policeman tells you to move your car, you will likely comply. You will not do so thinking, "Boy, I better move my car or he'll shoot me." Rather, "He's a policeman, I'll do what he says."

4. Expert Power. This is perhaps the antithesis of legitimate power. This power comes from the person, not the position. Earlier in this chapter we discussed the importance of having special abilities and knowledge. These are and examples of expert power. In a nutshell, it's that ability to do something important that others in the group can't do. Obviously there is a great advantage to this type of power, though it can take a long time to develop.

5. Referent Power. Referent power is the power that springs from relationships. Do you remember that Fielder identified interpersonal relationships as a critical leadership contingency? This is referent power.

To exert referent power the group members must like and respect you. For this reason it is probably the hardest type of power to establish. It is also the easiest type of power to lose. The act of using this type of power will likely undermine your relationship with your group members. If your boss asks you to work overtime as a personal favor, you might agree because you like her. If she makes a habit of it, however, you won't like her so much anymore. Use this power sparingly.

Following
By now, the line between leading and following should be sufficiently blurry. Much of what we've discussed in this chapter shows that leadership springs from all productive group members whether others acknowledge it or not. Your personal credibility should still be a concern, and there are certain linguistic behaviors that many of us fall into that undermine our leadership potential.

Have you noticed that powerful people just seem to act and talk differently from the rest of us? Bradac and Mulac (1984) identified six behaviors that powerless people engage in. They claimed that these linguistic behaviors severely undermine the credibility of those who use them in the eyes of listeners. These behaviors are:

1. **Hesitations.** Your public speaking teacher may have called these vocalized pauses. Using the statements, "Uh," "Um," "Ah," "You Know," etc., only undermine your perceived confidence in what you are saying.

2. **Hedges.** These are specific statements that weaken what we are about to say. "I guess," "I think," "It's only my opinion," "Basically," are all disclaimers. Again these statements make the listener think you don't really believe in what you are saying.

3. **Disclaimers.** A disclaimer goes beyond a hedge and tells the listener that what you are saying is some how flawed. "I know this will make you angry," "I'm probably wrong but," "I'm terrible at this stuff," are disclaimers and should be voided. Included in this category is the excessive use of apologies. If you truly have something to be sorry for, that's one thing, but don't apologize for things like disagreeing with someone.

4. **Tag questions.** This is turning a statement into a question, usually by tagging a phrase like, "Don't you agree?" or "Okay?" on

the end of a declarative statement. Which sounds more confident to you? "My report will be ready on Monday." "My report will be ready on Monday, okay?"

The use of powerless speech undermines your believability and overall credibility. The first step towards building your power base is to stop talking like a weak person.

Summary

In this chapter we examined the issue of leadership and its influence on the group process. We examined how people become leaders and how they exercise leadership and power. All in all, being a good leader is basically being a good group member. Anything you do that helps the group reach its goal is leadership. Though you won't always be recognized for your efforts, your work will likely have an influence.

References

Amsbary, J. (1986). *An examination of leadership emergence from a social Inference perspective.* Doctoral Dissertation: Indiana University.

Ambrose, S. (1994). *D-Day June 6, 1944: The climactic battle of World War II.* New York: Simon and Schuster.

Bennis, A., & Nanus, B. (1985). *Leaders: The strategies for taking charge.* New York: Harper and Row.

Blake, R., Mouton, J., & Allen, R. (1987). *Spectacular teamwork.* New York: Wiley & Sons.

Bradac, J. & Mulac, A. (1984). A molecular view of powerful and powerless speech styles: Attributional consequences of specific language features and communication intentions. *Communication Monographs, 51,* 307-319.

Bunyi J. (1985). Gender and leadership emergence: An experimental study. *Southern States Communication Journal, 50,* 246-260.

Burgoon, J. (1976). The ideal source: A re-examination of source credibility measurement. *Central States Speech Journal, 27,* 200-206.

Catell, R. (1951). New concepts for measuring leadership in terms of group syntality. *Human relations, 6,* 331-356.

Feidler, F. (1967). *A theory of leadership effectiveness.* New York: McGraw-Hill.

Gastil, J. (1994). A meta-analytic review of the productivity and satisfaction of democratic and autocratic leadership. *Small Group Research, 25,* 384-410.

Hickson, M., & Stacks, D. (1998). *Organizational communication in the personal context.* Boston: Allyn and Bacon.

Hollander, E., & Julian, J. (1970). Studies in leader legitimacy and innovation. In Berkowitz (ed.), *Advances in Experimental Social Psychology* (Vol. 5). New York: Academic Press.

Mausner, B., & Block, B. (1957). A study of additivity of variables affecting social interaction. *Journal of abnormal and social psychology, 54,* 250-256.

Mulder, M., & Wilke, H. (1970). Participation and power equalization. *Organizational behavior and human performance, 13,* 350-361.

Peters, T. (1987). *Thriving on chaos: Handbook for a management revolution.* New York: Random House.

Reicken, H. (1957). The effects of talkativenessand ability to influence group solutions of problems. *Sociometry, 21,* 309-321.

Ross, L., & Steinmetz, J. (1977). Social Role, social control, and biases in social-perception processes. *Journal of Personality and Social Psychology, 35,* 485-494.

Shaw, M.E. (1981). *Group dynamics: The psychology of small group behavior* (3rd ed). New York: McGraw Hill.

1. Leaders on Leading

Consider the following observations on what leadership is and what great leaders are. Can you find commonality among their opinions? Do you understand the process more or less?

> "Of the best rulers
> The people only know that they exist;
> The next best they love and praise; The next they fear;
> And the next they revile.
> When they do not command the people's faith,
> Some will lose faith in them
> And then they resort to oaths!
> But of the best when their task is accomplished,
> Their work done,
> The people all remark, "We have done it ourselves."
>
> —Lao-Tzu

"Don't tell people how to do things, tell them what to do and let them surprise you with their results."

—George S. Patton

"Leadership is the art of getting someone else to do something you want done because he wants to do it."

—Dwight Eisenhower

"Only one man in a thousand is a leader of men—the other 999 follow women."

—Groucho Marx

"It's hard to lead a cavalry charge if you think you look funny on a horse."

—Adlai Stevenson

"Inventories can be managed, but people must be led."

—H. Ross Perot

"Time is neutral and does not change things. With courage and initiative, leaders change things."

—Jesse Jackson

"If your actions inspire others to dream more, learn more, do more and become more, you are a leader."

—John Quincy Adams

"Cautious, careful people, always casting about to preserve their reputation and social standing, never can bring about a reform. Those who are really in earnest must be willing to be anything or nothing in the world's estimation, and publicly and privately, in season and out, avow their sympathy with despised and persecuted ideas and their advocates, and bear the consequences."

—Susan B. Anthony

"Leaders aren't born, they are made. And they are made just like anything else, through hard work. And that's the price we'll have to pay to achieve that goal, or any goal."

—Vince Lombardi

"The price of greatness is responsibility."

—Winston Churchill

"Dignity does not consist in possessing honors, but in deserving them."

—Aristotle

2. Leaders in the Twentieth Century

In 1998, *Time* Magazine listed the twenty political or revolutionary leaders that most shaped the twentieth century. Do you agree with this list? Who would you add/deleted and why?

> David Ben-Gurion
> Ho Chi Minh
> Winston Churchill
> Mohandas Gandhi
> Mikhail Gorbachev
> Adolf Hitler
> Martin Luther King
> Ayatullah Ruhollah Khomeini
> V.I. Lenin
> Nelson Mandela
> Pope John Paul II
> Ronald Reagan
> Eleanor Roosevelt
> Franklin Delano Roosevelt
> Teddy Roosevelt
> Margaret Thatcher
> Unknown Rebel
> Margaret Sanger
> Lech Walesa
> Mao Zedong

From the Dec. 8, 1998 issue of TIME magazine

3. "Come-With Guys."

We spend a lot of time discussing how leaders can be overbearing and demanding. How they can pull a group one way or another. Sometimes though, groups can run amok without a leader's help. Consider the following:

When I first lived in Birmingham I had a circle of friends left over from my years in college. Some lived here in town and others were in the military and stationed close by. During this time the movie *Terminator 2* came out and we all decided that we wanted to see it and that we wanted to see it together. I wasn't willing to wait, however, so I went to see the film alone, privately promising that "It's okay, I'll just see it again when everyone is back in town."

When we did get back together we all headed off to see the movie and it wasn't until we got out that one of my friends (who knew I had broken the covenant and had seen the movie on my own) said, "Wow Jonathan, you must really love that movie!"

"Not really," I replied. "I was just being a come-with guy."

Another of my friends chimed in, "You're kidding, I already saw it and was only coming to be with you guys too!"

It soon became clear that none of us really wanted to see the movie again, we were just coming along.

Did this group have a leader? Do groups have to have leaders? How often to you behave because you *think* everyone else wants something but you're not really sure?

CHAPTER 10

MEETINGS WITH PURPOSE

Meetings are scheduled for a variety of reasons: *dissemination or sharing of information, delegating of tasks, decision making, or problem-solving.* Recognizing the goal of the meeting is necessary for the group to proceed efficiently. A prepared group leader will inform the group members about the purpose of the meeting ahead of time, but often participants are not aware of the purpose or goal of a meeting until they arrive, if even then. Common complaints about meetings with unclear goals sound like this: "We go around and around an never accomplish anything," "no one seems to know what we're doing here," or "another meeting, another waste of my time." The purpose of this chapter is to help a participant identify the group's goal and help the group effectively and efficiently achieve it.

At the beginning of every meeting the leader should state the goal or purpose of the meeting, even if everyone already has been told, so that all group members will be 'on the same page.' If there is not a designated leader, then the group shares responsibility in getting started. Someone should take the initiative and ask the group what is the perceived goal of the meeting. Then a discussion can follow with all members arriving at a defined goal together.

Meetings that have a goal of *sharing information* leaves the individual member with the task of deciding if he or she is the recipient or the supplier of the desired information, or possibly both. If a supervisor simply has information to share with a specific group, then a memo would be more appropriate than a meeting. More than likely, if a meeting was scheduled, then a discussion is expected. Hopefully, each member that was expected to participate was given forewarning so they may be prepared to contribute pertinent data. As information is exchanged among several or all of the members, and the goal of exchanging information is reached, the meeting should be adjourned. The meeting time is directly related to the amount of information that should be disseminated. A focus on the goal of the meeting will help keep the length of the meeting to a minimum.

Meetings that have a purpose of *delegating tasks* are usually called to make sure that all the jobs that produce the organization's specific product will get done by someone. With a task, there is no doubt about what is to be done or how to go about doing it. It's just a matter of who is going to do it. But, if a the boss wants certain individuals to do certain tasks, then a meeting is not justified. Assignments can be made without necessitating a group discussion. But, scheduling a meeting to solicit volunteers for specific tasks is common. A listing of the tasks followed by individuals volunteering to do the tasks accomplishes the purpose of the meeting. The meeting can end. But, perhaps a supervisor needs help in deciding who should be assigned to different tasks. He may then call a meeting of fellow supervisors to discuss recommendations.

Now the purpose of the meeting is not to delegate but to make a decision. *Decision making* can be defined as a process of making reasoned choices from several alternatives. If the choices are clear, the discussion results in a decision, or series of decisions fairly quickly. The meeting has served it's purpose and can be adjourned. But if choices are not easy and none of the alternatives seem acceptable, the group has a problem. A *problem* is a blocked goal. A *goal* is a human desire toward which one is willing to work. A small group goal is a human desire toward which all members are willing to work. Problems arise when there is indecision of how to proceed to overcome barriers that prevent attainment of an agreed upon goal. A problem is a question of what should be done, and how it should be done (Smith, 1965).

Thinking about a problem is difficult for an individual and certainly for groups unless an orderly approach is used. Unless the group agrees on some order, a way to proceed together, profitable and efficient group thinking is nearly impossible. A traditional pattern of inquiry used in group problem-solving is the process of *reflective thinking* previously discussed in Chapter 4. It is a pattern based on John Dewey's analysis of how we think when we are confronted with a problem, and it bears repeating here. This process is effective when the leader and group members have some training in the method and are willing to work toward a common goal. It works best in a group of three to eight people but can be rather time consuming, committing the group to a series of meetings. Communication experts differ in their adaptations of Dewey's approach. This six step process is one of those adaptations.

Traditional Pattern of Problem-solving
(1) Define the problem
(2) Analyze the problem
(3) Establish criteria for the solution
(4) Propose solutions
(5) Analyze solutions and select the best
(6) Develop a plan to implement the solution

As the group discusses the problem in each step of the process, it is working toward a solution that takes into account differing perceptions, differing areas of expertise and knowledge of the group members. A series of decisions will be made together. The initial steps allow the group to decide if the problem warrants further discussion. Each step paves the way for agreement on the solution. If the group reaches a final decision by consensus, the solution will be supported long after the discussion is over, therefore having a better chance of being implemented. *Consensus* occurs when all group members agree on a solution. Consensus not only strengthens the group but unifies it. increases the potential for implementing the solutions. Consensus, however, requires effective communication, recognition of a common goal, a supportive communication climate, and a great deal of time (Hickson, 1998).

To begin, members should think of problem solving as an open-ended inquiry. This would dictate that the group members assume an investigative posture, a mind set of openness, a willingness to look at all possibilities, thus paving the way for consensus. The group spends much of their time posing questions to each other and providing answers. Personal agendas and preconceived ideas of the solution become minimized. The group goal becomes preeminent.

Step 1. Define the Problem
In the first step, the group determines exactly *what* problem warrants discussion. Groups should realize that everyone's understanding of

the problem will vary, so in order to have a collective train of thought, the group begins to define the problem systematically.

1. What is our goal?
2. Word the problem as and open-ended question including the stated goal.
3. Define terms in the formulated question and other concepts that may need to be clarified for common understanding.
4. Agree that a problem does exist and it warrants further discussion.

For instance, a group of partners of a firm are meeting because they have a perceived problem within their support staff. Complaints have been circulating around the office and two people have resigned resulting in low morale.

1. They begin their discussion by identifying their goal. They might decide their goal is 'job satisfaction' of their support staff.
2. To word their problem for discussion they could formulate a question: "How can we provide job satisfaction for our support staff?" or "What can be done to insure job satisfaction for our support staff?" The question is not limited to a yes or no answer.
3. The partners define the terms that the group will be discussing. What do we mean by 'job satisfaction', and who do we include in 'support staff'? Other concepts they clarify: Do we want *every* person *completely* satisfied? Do we want to think of the support staff as a *group* that we are *approximating* job satisfaction for?
4. The group asks the question: "Do we actually have a problem that we will commit to solving?" The partners agree that the problem does exist and they should grapple with it immediately. But, if the partners, after careful thought realize they cannot agree on a common goal or can't agree that anything should be done, then pursuing this method of problem-solving would be a waste of time. The group can consider an alternative method to solve the problem which will be discussed later in this chapter.

Step 2. Analyze the Problem
In the second step the group looks at the scope of the problem and its importance.

1. What are the symptoms of the problem and causes of the problem?

2. Who is affected besides the group?

3. Will the situation improve itself or become worse if nothing is done?

4. What has been done previously, if anything, to solve the problem? Was it effective? If not, why not?

5. Identify other barriers to the goal (other than recognized causes) such as social, political, or financial factors.

6. What areas must be corrected now and what should be excluded from this particular discussion?

7. What further information is critical to be able to fully understand the nature of the problem?

The partners of the firm are ready to proceed by analyzing the problem as they understand it from step 1.

1. They isolate *symptoms* of job dissatisfaction as multiple complaints, uncooperative attitudes, staff coming in late or leaving early, and bickering among themselves. They now recognize *causes* of the problem as unevenly distributed perks, too narrowly defined job descriptions, sticking to the personnel policies with some but not everyone, lack of resources to complete assigned tasks, and differing levels of expectations from the partners.

2. The partners may realize that this situation is affecting their clients as well. A client recently asked "What is going on down here? Previously when I called, I usually got whatever I asked for very quickly."

3. The partners agree the problem has become urgent. Things will get worse if they do not intervene.

4. The previous pep talks to the staff are just a band aid.

5. There may be other barriers to the goals other than the causes. Perhaps politically, there are some territorial issues with staff that have seniority. To rearrange office space, equipment, job requirements, or supervisory roles may inflame some staff. Also, financial resources may be limited and there won't be much money for solving the problem.

6. The partners then ask "What do we try to solve now and what will be excluded from our discussion?" Interestingly enough most of the staff are not complaining about their salaries, so the group decides to exclude that from the discussion and concentrate on the most prevalent complaints. They list the urgent areas of the problem that must be solved.

The group is now ready for the step 3, thinking about the criteria the solution should meet. After attempting to analyze the problem the group may decide to adjourn until further research can be done in order to fully understand the complexities of the problem. The group may want to allow the members to have time to weigh issues that have been covered. When the group reconvenes, it can pick up where it left off, after a brief review.

Let's consider another scenario. After analyzing the problem, they find that the source of the complaints and most of the dissatisfaction existed with the two employees that have already left. Low morale is a result of the shake-up following the two resignations and is judged to be temporary. The remaining staff seem happy in their jobs. A problem no longer exists and the discussion can be terminated.

Volkema and Gorman describe the first two steps as the formulation of the problem. Gathering information in order to define or describe the perceived problem is essential in preventing a group from committing an 'error of the third kind', essentially, solving the wrong problem (Yadav, 1985). Groups that exhibit substantial formulation activity have been found to have more efficient problem-solving experiences and make better decisions. Groups have a tendency to rush through these phases of the process because they erroneously assume that everyone already understands the problem. The group narrows the scope of the problem and focuses on solutions prematurely (Volkema, 1995). It is very tempting to jump to a discussion of solutions because the cause and effect relationship between the goal and the barriers often reveals what should be done. The group must be willing to invest the time it takes to effectively utilize these first two steps and initiate self discipline in order to be thorough. A group will be more likely to agree on a solution for a problem if it first adequately understands the problem.

Step 3. Establish Criteria for the Solution
Criteria are guidelines, boundaries, standards, or rules that a group agrees to follow in reaching a solution to their problem. Setting criteria for the solution at this point in the discussion helps the group to be unbiased and objective about certain solutions that will come up later (Hamilton, 1997). Graham, Papa, and McPherson (1997) found that groups that have a clear standard of what constitutes a high quality decision before they evaluate possible solutions have a

chance of having a more effective process and a superior solution. The group decides together on the criteria by which they will judge the solution.

1. What must the solution do?
2. What must the solution avoid?
3. What restrictions of time, money, politics, etc. must be considered?
4. Rank the criteria from most important to least important.

In this step the partners with the support staff problem now set the criteria for the solution.

1. The group agrees that the solution should remove the causes of the problem: evenly distribute the perks, re-write job descriptions that all partners honor, be consistent in applying personnel policies, provide everyone with satisfactory resources and equipment to meet the job description.
2. The solution should not down-size the staff, it should be presented to the staff as an option they can modify through feedback.
3. The solution should not alienate the senior staff. Implementation of the solution should begin right away. New equipment can't cost any more money than what's currently available.
4. They rank their criteria to prioritize them for use in the next step, analyzing solutions.

Step 4. Propose Solutions
The group suggests a wide range of possible solutions and records them so the whole group can see them. The goal at this point is a long list of all possibilities, not a list of high quality solutions (Smith, 1965).

1. Appoint a secretary and list all possible solutions.
2. Group the solutions according to similarity so they may be easily discussed.
3. Refrain from discussing pros and cons of suggested solutions at this point.

One way to obtain a creative lists of ideas is brainstorming. It is a technique that encourages all members to think freely an contribute the range of options. *Brainstorming* is a method of suggesting ideas quickly and spontaneously in random order until ideas are exhausted. Brainstorming is advantageous in that the members of a group stimulate each other's imaginations, and build on one another's ideas. All members should participate, jumping in with a possible solution as they think of it. By listing all suggestions on a chalkboard, flip chart, or transparency, the group can easily review the list together for categorizing the suggested solutions. Be sure someone in the group makes a copy of the list before you leave the meeting if it was recorded on a chalkboard.

For effective brainstorming, the group refrains from judging each solution as it is made. Criticism of solutions is suspended until the next step of the problem-solving process. The only comments allowed should be words of encouragement or requests for clarification of an idea. Members are more likely to contribute if they know their ideas won't be shot down immediately. Research has shown that the quality of both individual and group decisions are improved when open exchanges of information, ideas, and criticism are allowed (Burleson, 1984).

Our partners working on their staff problem proceed to brainstorm possible solutions. They categorized them by the causes each solution will remove. For example, they listed possible solutions for making perks even for everyone, listed possible solutions for re-writing job descriptions, an so on.

Nominal Group Technique. If brainstorming is proving to be fruitless because one or two members are monopolizing the time, or some members seem reluctant to participate, or there are long pauses in between suggestions, then another procedure may be more effective. The *nominal group technique* (NGT) can be used to generate ideas (Delbecq 1986). First, solutions are silently generated by each member and written down privately. The secretary then records one idea from each member as he goes around the group until all ideas are on the board, including ones that members thought of while others were talking. As with brainstorming, only discussion to clarify meaning or to list group suggestions is allowed. Each member then privately selects the top 5 or 6 ideas and ranks them according to preference. Votes are then recorded on the chalkboard. The group selects the top ideas.

Brainstorming and NGT are techniques used for generating a list of ideas. They are useful in any step of the traditional process where lists of ideas are desired. Both of these techniques do not allow for criticism and evaluation of ideas as they are given so they are not effective decision making methods.

Step 5. Analyze Solutions

The group may find that as they evaluate each proposed solution that this step of the process is easier than expected. They already have a clear understanding of causes of the problem, other barriers to the goal, a wide range of options to choose from, and a criteria for the solution. The ground work has been laid.

    1. Read through the list of possibilities discussing strengths and weaknesses of each.

    2. Discuss each of the solutions in light of its ability to meet the criteria, remove causes of the problem or barriers to the goal.

    3. Make a list the best solutions until one solution evolves or a combination of solutions.

    4. Which objectionable features of the approved solution or solutions should be modified?

Because problems are complicated, solutions may range from outright removal of a barrier or cause or to the revision of the goal in light of an immovable barrier. Researchers have found that it is important to positively evaluate decision alternatives instead of quickly eliminating them off of a list. When group members focus on the positive characteristic of decision alternatives a more constructive climate for interaction occurs. Groups tend to go immediately to a 'process of elimination' and often overlook the potential of some solutions. (Graham, Papa, Mcpherson, 1997).

The best solution will be one reached by *consensus*, where all members are in agreement. Realistically there times when a compromise is the best case scenario. The last resort would be a vote, if a decision has to be made and time has run out. Voting divides the group at the end of a lengthy process and the solution will not be implemented with solid support from the group.

A group that strives for consensus at all cost, however, can jeopardize the spirit of inquiry. This is a pitfall of small groups known as groupthink. *Groupthink* is a phenomenon described by Irving Janis where a group desires to avoid conflict at the expense of critical thinking. The group considers reaching agreement more important that careful consideration of alternatives, and individuals feel the pressure to conform (Janis, 1988). Groupthink almost always yields negative results. The group, unable to fully understand the problem and its consequences, will find the group's plans are inadequate and consequently fail (Hickson, 1998).

Ways to Avoid Groupthink (Hamilton, 1997)
At the initial meeting the leader can set the stage for open disagreemnt by explaining the "agree to disagree" rule for the group. She can model the desired approach for the group.

- Bring in outside experts with differing opinions
- To keep from influencing the group, the leader (particularly if she is in an authoritative role) should keep personal opinions to herself until others have expressed theirs.
- She can remove herself from the group.
- Once a tentative solution has been reached, she can give members a "second chance" to rethink their choice and to discuss any doubts they have.

While most groups seek to divorce themselves from conflict, open and honest disagreement is often the best cure for both conflict and groupthink (Hickson, 1998).

The partners of our firm have come up with a combination of solutions. They will re-write job descriptions for all support staff, they agreed to apply personnel policies evenly, and agreed to eliminate favoritism. They will supply a computer(used) for each cubicle and enough printed resources for all staff. They will communicate changes to the staff before they are implemented.

Step 6. Develop a Plan to Implement the Solution
For some problems, the implementation procedure is clear because it is implied in the solution chosen. For some problems implementing the solution becomes the greatest difficulty of all. This step of the process becomes the most important one. A satisfied group may take their decision to upper management and be met with the reaction: "That's wonderful, who's going to do it?, or who's going to pay for it?" To have a well thought out plan may make the difference between a decision that has become a waste of the group members' time in the boardroom and a problem actually getting solved. If the group judges their solution to be impractical they can return to step 5 and select another solution that may be more practical to implement.

The group may have been given the power to initiate the implementation. In that case, decisions concerning how to carry out each phase of the plan and who will actually carry out each phase can now be made.

Our partners now delegate tasks. They decide who will be re-writing the job descriptions and an appropriate frame to expect it to be finished, who will shop for computers, who will order the print resources, and so on. A joint meeting with the support staff was scheduled.

For the traditional problem-solving method to perform at its best, all participants need to take responsibility for the group's success. Everyone needs to do research, give all members a chance to discuss, ensure contributions are timely, periodically summarize the group's progress, and evaluate ideas critically, not personalities. The traditional problem-solving method works best when the leader and group members are trained in how to use the method, when the group is very small (3-8 members, seated in a circle), and when the members have time to prepare. Other techniques may be used when the traditional problem-solving pattern does not have a chance to work. Single-question procedure, ideal-solution procedure, Delphi, or buzz groups have proved successful in problem-solving.

Single-Question Procedure

C.E. Larson (1969) outlines these five steps:

1) What is the single question, the answer to which is all that the group needs to know to accomplish its purpose?

2). What subquestions must be answered before we can answer the single question we have formulated?

3) Do we have sufficient information to answer confidently the subquestions? If no, continue below.

4) What are the most reasonable answers to the subquestions?

5) Assuming that our answers to the subquestions are correct, what is the best solution to the problem?

Ideal Solution Procedure

The ideal-solution is an alternative to the single-question procedure and may be helpful when members' feelings are likely to run high (Hamilton, 1997).

1. Are we all agreed on the nature of the problem?

2. What would be the ideal solution from the point of view of all parties involved in the problem?

173

3. What conditions within the problem could be changed so that the ideal solution might be achieved?

4. Of the solutions available to us, which one best approximates the ideal solution?

The Delphi Technique (Dalkey, 1969)

There are times when conflict or extreme disagreement make Dewey's traditional method of problem-solving problematic. Delphi groups do not meet, but correspond instead. This can reduce the potential for personality and leadership conflicts as well as avoiding groupthink. In the *Delphi Technique* someone chooses the group and establishes lines of communication. The leader defines the task in writing and members respond via memo. Each group member's position is then paraphrased and returned for all to evaluate and respond. At some point in time the leader should summarize the group's decisions to date. This process continues until the group reaches consensus on a solution. With this technique, some excellent ideas may be lost due to the inability to "tag" one idea upon another (Hickson,1998).

The Buzz Group

The Buzz Group Technique can work even when members are not well informed about the problem or the leader is not trained in problem-solving. The buzz group is appropriate when the group is too large for a traditional problem-solving method. An expert briefs the large group on the nature of the problem expanding the participants' knowledge of the problem. The large group divides into buzz groups of five to eight people and are instructed to discuss the problem, formulate suggestions, and report back to the whole group. Hamilton describes one variation of buzz group procedures.

1. Divide the large group into small groups.
2. Have each group appoint a timekeeper.
3. Have each group appoint a secretary to record ideas.
4. Have each group state the specific topic to be discussed.
5. Have each group member take 1 minute to express opinions.
6. Have each group take 5 minutes (or more) to discuss its list and to select (by consensus) the best one or two ideas or suggestions.
7. Have each recorder report the group's conclusions to the large group.
8. Follow up with a general discussion by all those present.

When time is limited, a list of ideas or solutions can be handed out to buzz groups. Each buzz group discusses the list and ranks the solutions or selects the best solution.

Granted, all of these techniques and methods of decision making and problem solving have been described under optimum conditions. In reality you will encounter groups that are attempting to solve problems with no recognizable plan. You will find yourself in groups that are attempting to discuss issues without a clear goal. How can you be instrumental in turning things around? Remember a few basic requirements for successful groups. The first is a stated goal. You can ask that question. When the goal is reached the meeting should adjourn. You can suggest that, if the group has not realized it. Effective groups have an orderly approach. If the group is floundering, suggest an approach. All group members are valuable participants. You can encourage others to contribute. Groupthink is counterproductive. You can be willing to express honest disagreement with ideas but not personalities. A spirit of inquiry encourages participation. Ask questions.

Frustrations with people and processes occur frequently in small group communication and are probably inevitable. If you know a few basics, you can at least reduce the frustration level not only for you but the rest of the group and actually be instrumental in the group reaching its goal.

Summary
Groups can be useful and valuable tools within any formal or informal organization, but they can also become a frustrating waste of time. Dissatisfaction with groups seems to be growing, with an increasingly number of people viewing them negatively. However, by understanding the basics of group discussion techniques and the limitations of the process, you can make your meetings more successful. You can survive group meetings and still be happy with the process.

References
Dalkey, N. C. (June, 1969). The delphi method: An experimental study of group opinion. Rand Corporation Memorandum RM 5888-PR.

Delbecq, A. L., Van de Ven, A. H., & Gustasfson, D. H. (1986). *Group techniques for program planning: A guide to nominal group and delphi process.* Westport, CT: Briar Press.

Graham, E. E., Papa , M. J., & McPherson, M. B. (1997). An applied test of the functional communication perspective of small group decision-making. *Southern Communication Journal, 62(4),* 269-279.

Hamilton, C. (1997). *Communicating for results: A guide for business & the professions* (5th ed.). Belmont, CA: Wadsworth.

Janis, I. L. (1998). *Crucial decisions: Leadership in policy making & crisis management.* New York: Free Press.

Larson, C. E. (1969). Forms of analysis and small group problem-solving. *Speech Monographs, 36.*

Smith, W. S. (1966). *Group problem-solving through discussion: A process essential to democracy* (2nd ed.). Indianapolis: Bobbs-Merrill.

Volkema, R. J. (1995). Creativity in MS/OR managing the process of formulating the problem. *Interfaces, 25(3),* 81-87.

Volkema, R. J. & Gorman, R. H. (1998). The influence of cognitive-based group composition on decision-making process and outcome. *Journal of Management Studies, 35(1),* 105-117.

Yadav, S. B. & Korukonda, A. (1985). Management of type III error in problem identification. *Interfaces, 15(4),* 55-61.